THE SCIENCES OF COGNITION

THE SCIENCES OF COGNITION

COGNITION

THEORY AND RESEARCH IN PSYCHOLOGY AND ARTIFICIAL INTELLIGENCE

Morton Wagman

Westport, Connecticut
London

Library of Congress Cataloging-in-Publication Data

Wagman, Morton.
      The sciences of cognition : theory and research in psychology and
artificial intelligence / Morton Wagman.
           p.   cm.
      Includes bibliographical references and index.
      ISBN 0–275–94948–6 (alk. paper)
      1. Cognitive science. 2. Artificial intelligence. 3. Cognition.
4. Cognitive psychology. 5. Intellect. I. Title.
BF311.W2659   1995
153—dc20   94–28001

British Library Cataloguing in Publication Data is available.

Library of Congress Catalog Card Number: 94–28001
ISBN: 0–275–94948–6

First published in 1995

Praeger Publishers, 88 Post Road West, Westport, CT 06881
An imprint of Greenwood Publishing Group, Inc.

Printed in the United States of America

The paper used in this book complies with the
Permanent Paper Standard issued by the National
Information Standards Organization (Z39.48–1984).

10 9 8 7 6 5 4 3 2 1

Copyright Acknowledgments

The author and publisher are grateful for permission to reprint from the following:

Extracts from pp. 582, 584–596, and 619–621 and Figures 1, 2, 10a, and 10b of Elio, R.
and Scharf, P. (1990). Modeling novice-to-expert shifts in problem solving strategy and
knowledge organization. *Cognitive Science, 14,* 576–639. Reprinted with the
permission of Ablex Publishing Corporation.

Extract from pp. 272–277 of Holyoak, K. J. and Spellman, B. A. (1993). Thinking.
Annual Review of Psychology, 44, 265–315. Copyright © 1993 by Annual Reviews,
Inc. Reproduced with permission.

Extracts from pp. 295, 306–312, 318, 340–341, and 344–347 and Tables 2, 4, and 16 of
Holyoak, K. J. and Thagard, P. (1989). Analogical mapping by constraint satisfaction.

Contents

Illustrations

FIGURES

Preface

This book examines the nature of intelligence and intelligent systems as revealed by the sciences of psychology and artificial intelligence.

In the first chapter, the central and detailed aspects of a general unified theory of intelligence are presented. Unitary theories of human and artificial cognition are discussed in depth. The foundations and objectives of artificial intelligence are examined. The scope and limits of the SOAR system as a theory of unified cognition are discussed. The major sources, objectives, and approaches of cognitive psychology are analyzed.

In the second chapter, theories of reasoning and its computational modeling are considered. Experimental research in human reasoning is described, and the results are interpreted from the perspectives of several theories of deduction.

In the third chapter, problem solving and its computational modeling are considered. Theory and research concerned with the interrelationships of strategic approach and knowledge organization in problem solving are examined. Problem representation and problem solving in the EUREKA program are analyzed in terms of EUREKA's expert and novice protocols.

In the fourth chapter, the nature of analogical thinking is discussed. The ACME model of analogical mapping and its applications to a formal mathematical analogy and to a literary metaphor are examined in depth.

In the fifth, and final, chapter, scientific discovery processes in the context of artificial intelligence and human psychology are discussed.

The processes by which BACON.3 achieved its scientific discoveries are described. BACON.3's rediscovery of Kepler's third law of planetary motion is compared with its rediscovery by university students in the setting of a laboratory experiment and with the original discovery by Kepler. The chapter concludes with an analysis of the nature of discovery and its relation to a general theory of intelligence.

The book is directed toward graduate and advanced undergraduate students in psychology, artificial intelligence, and cognitive science. Scholars and professionals in these and related disciplines will also find the book useful.

Acknowledgments

I am grateful to LaDonna Wilson for her excellent work in assisting with all aspects of the preparation of the manuscript. I also thank Ann Schlosser, Kimberly Pollack, and Annette Deetz for their excellent typing of portions of the manuscript.

1

The Nature of Intelligence and Intelligent Systems

GENERAL UNIFIED THEORY OF INTELLIGENCE

Central Aspects of the Theory

A different, more abstract, and inclusive general unified theory of intelligence can be formulated on the basis of the logic of implication. This fundamental theorem of intelligence would hold that the logic of implication (if p, then q) subsumes both the formal structure of human reasoning and problem solving and the formal structure of artificial intelligence. The logic of implication is foundational to mathematical and scientific reasoning and to the reasoning of everyday behavior (Wagman, 1978, 1984, 1993) and is foundational to programming logic and knowledge representation formalisms in artificial intelligence systems (Wagman, 1980, 1988, 1991a, 1991b).

Mathematics and Unified Theories in Science

Mathematics summarizes scientific research results, but, more significantly, mathematics formulates general bodies of scientific theory.

Mathematics is the foundation of all exact knowledge of natural phenomena (Hilbert, quoted in Kline, 1985, p. vi).

Unified Electromagnetic Theory

The mathematical equations of Maxwell constitute the complete and precise formulation of the theory of electromagnetism. An immense range of physical phenomena is unified mathematically.

The mathematical equations have profound significance. The equations unify the diverse phenomena in the radiation spectrum, and deductions from the equations describe and predict empirical results of experiments and applications. Physical explanation is by means of mathematical symbols. "In Maxwell's theory an electric charge is but the recipient of a symbol" (Helmholtz, quoted in Kline, 1985, p. 146). "The originality of mathematics consists in the fact that in the mathematical sciences connections between things are exhibited which, apart from the agency of human reason, are extremely unobvious" (Whitehead, quoted in Kline, 1985, p. 141).

Unified Newtonian Theory

The Newtonian theory is a mathematical theory that describes and predicts by means of its equations the terrestrial and celestial behavior of physical bodies. The mathematical equations and deductions from them are universal. Newton's equation for the force of attraction between two masses includes a gravitational constant, but the concept of gravitation itself is not well understood.

The Newtonian equations and their derivations are basic to the contemporary scientific exploration of space, but their extraordinary scope and power were already known in the eighteenth-century mathematical work of Lagrange and Laplace.

We have given, in the first part of this work, the general principles of the equilibrium and motion of bodies. The application of these principles to the motions of the heavenly bodies had conducted us, by geometrical reasoning, without any hypothesis, to the law of universal attraction, the action of gravity and the motion of projectiles being particular cases of this law. We have taken into consideration a system of bodies subjected to this great law of nature and have obtained, by a singular analysis, the general expressions of their motions, of their figures, and of the oscillations of the fluids which cover them. From these expressions we have deduced all the known phenomena of the flow and ebb of the tide; the variations of the degrees and the force of gravity at the surface of the earth; the precession of the equinoxes; the libration of the moon; and the figure and rotation of Saturn's rings. We have also pointed out the cause that these rings remain permanently in the plane of the equator of Saturn.

Moreover we have deduced, from the same theory of gravity, the principle equations of the motions of the planets, particularly those of Jupiter and Saturn, whose great inequalities have a period of above 900 years [Laplace, quoted in Kline, 1985, p. 119].

Regarding the law of gravitation, Newton himself emphasized that it was a mathematical law, a computational law, and not one based on complete knowledge of the nature of gravitation itself.

So far I have explained the phenomena of the heavens and of the sea by the force of gravity. . . . I have not yet been able to deduce from the phenomena the reasons for these properties of gravity and I invent no hypothesis [*hypotheses no fingo*]. For everything which is not deduced from the phenomena should be called a hypothesis, and hypotheses, whether metaphysical or physical, whether occult qualities or mechanical, have no place in experimental philosophy. In this philosophy propositions are deduced from phenomena and rendered general by induction. . . . It is enough that gravity really exists, that it acts according to the laws we have set out and that it suffices for all the movements of the heavenly bodies and of the sea [Newton, quoted in Kline, 1985, p. 121].

Unified Einsteinian Theory

Einsteinian theory subsumes Newtonian theory. However, the concept of weight due to gravitational force is eliminated. Mass is considered as inertial mass in the two Newtonian equations.

The Newtonian concept of three dimensional Euclidean space is replaced by curved four dimensional space time. In Einsteinian theory, observed measurements may vary as a function of the relative location of the observer and relative motions of frames of reference. The mathematical theory involves equations of Riemannian differential geometry and the equations of tensor analysis; the former relate to the nature of Einsteinian space, the latter to the equalization of varying observers and frames of reference. Tensor analysis provided to Einstein a mathematical basis for his unified theory of relativity: "The general laws of nature are to be expressed by equations which hold good for all systems of coordinates" (Einstein, quoted in Kline, 1985, p. 163).

Logical Structure and the Reality of the General Unified Theory of Intelligence

The architecture of the general unified theory of intelligence is constructed on the foundation stone of the logic of implication that supports conceptual elements in both natural intelligence and artificial intelligence. The architecture coordinates a remote abstract logical structure on the one hand and the palpable evidential behavior of human and computer reasoning and problem solving on the other hand. The concrete reality of the latter is brought under the explanatory aegis of the former. Mathematical logical symbols preside over and give the best explanation of cognition. This precedence of logic seems counter intuitive; yet, there is a clear and illuminating analogy in the relationship between logic and physics, as summarized by Albert Einstein.

According to Newton's system, physical reality is characterized by the concepts of space, time, material point, and force (reciprocal action of material points).

. . .

After Maxwell they conceived physical reality as represented by continuous fields, not mechanically explicable, which are subject to partial differential equations. This change in the conception of reality is the most profound and fruitful one that has come to physics since Newton.

. . .

The view I have just outlined of the purely fictitious character of the fundamentals of scientific theory was by no means the prevailing one in the 18th and 19th centuries. But it is steadily gaining ground from the fact that *the distance in thought between the fundamental concepts and laws on one side, and, on the other, the conclusions which have to be brought into relation with our experience grows larger and larger, the simpler the logical structure becomes — that is to say, the smaller the number of logically independent conceptual elements which are found necessary to support the structure* [italics added] [Einstein, 1931].

The Intelligence of Mathematics

The ancient Pythagoreans proclaimed with awe, "All is number." Heinrich Hertz, who developed the theory and technology of radio waves, asserted that electromagnetic wave phenomena were best understood as mathematical equations and, like Pythagoras, believed that mathematics had an intrinsic intelligence of its own that sometimes surpassed its creators.

Hertz said, "Maxwell's theory consists of Maxwell's equations." There is no mechanical explanation, and there is no need for one. He continued, "One cannot escape the feeling that these equations have an existence and an intelligence of their own, that they are wiser than we are, even than their discoverers, that we get more out of them than we originally put into them" (Kline, 1985, p. 144).

Logical Implication and Mathematical Proof

The first known application of the logical implication argument *reductio ad absurdum* to the establishment of mathematical proofs was made by Euclid around 300 B.C. In the *reductio ad absurdum* argument, there are three steps in the establishment of the truth of a mathematical proposition: (1) assume the proposition is false, (2) demonstrate that the implication of this assumption leads to a contradiction, and (3) conclude on the grounds of the contradiction that the proposition is true. Euclid used this method to establish the truth of the proposition that the square root of two is an irrational number.

During the centuries following Euclid, mathematicians have established the truth or falsehood of many mathematical conjectures by means of the *reductio ad absurdum* argument.

In 1993, the mathematical conjecture known as "Fermat's last theorem" was proven to be true (Kolata, 1993). Fermat had advanced his conjecture in the seventeenth century, but its establishment had eluded generations of the world's best mathematicians. Fermat proposed that the equation $x^n + y^n = z^n$, where x, y, and z are integers, has no solution for values of n greater than two.

In a lecture given at Cambridge University before an assemblage of renowned mathematicians in June 1993, Andrew Wiles of Princeton University proved by means of the *reductio ad absurdum* argument that Fermat's conjecture was true.

Clearly, the establishment of Wiles' proof, like the establishment of Euclid's proof, required, in addition to the *reductio ad absurdum* method, technical mathematical knowledge (elementary algebra in the case of Euclid, advanced algebraic geometry and other topics in the case of Wiles). The *reductio ad absurdum* argument is, however, a sine qua non.

The Intelligence of Computer Programs

In their proof of the Four Color Theorem, Appel and Haken (1979) found, to their surprise, that their computer program made intellectual contributions to their complex work and displayed an original intelligence that sometimes surpassed their own.

In early 1975 we modified [the] experimental program to yield obstacle-free configurations and forced it to search for arguments that employed configurations of small ring size. The resulting runs pointed out the need for new improvements in the procedure, but also yielded a very pleasant surprise:

replacing geographically good configurations by obstacle-free ones did not seem to more than double the size of the unavoidable set.

At this point the program, which has by now absorbed our ideas and improvements for two years, began to surprise us. At the beginning we would check its arguments by hand so we could always predict the course it would follow in any situation; but now it suddenly started to act like a chess-playing machine. It would work out compound strategies based on all the tricks it had been "taught" and often these approaches were far more clever than those we would have tried. Thus it began to teach us things about how to proceed that we never expected. In a sense it had surpassed its creators in some aspects of the "intellectual" as well as the mechanical parts of the task [italics added] [Appel and Haken, 1979, p. 175].

Intelligence and Nature

The works of Newton, Maxwell, and Einstein have rendered nature mathematically comprehensible. Inherent in mathematics and in computer programs there appears to be, as discussed in the previous two sections, an order of intelligence that "is wiser than we are, wiser even than their discoverers" (Hertz, quoted in Kline, 1985) and that "surpassed its creators in some aspects of the intellectual as well as the mechanical parts of the task" (Appel and Haken, 1979). The human mind has created both mathematical intelligence and artificial intelligence, and though these creations may seem to provide inevitable and singular truths about nature, these truths are arbitrary constructions and the result of our own cognitive projections.

[We] have found that where science has progressed the farthest, the mind has but regained from nature that which the mind has put into nature. We have found a strange foot print on the shore of the unknown. We have devised profound theories, one after another, to account for its origin. At last, we have succeeded in reconstructing the creature that made the footprint. And Lo! it is our own [Eddington, 1933].

It is of interest that Sir Arthur Stanley Eddington (1882–1944), who, in 1919, confirmed by astronomical measurements predictions derived from Einstein's theory of relativity, hypothesized that because knowledge of the universe is the product of the human mind, discovery of the nature of the mechanics of the human mind would enable purely conceptual procedures to formulate the entire science of physics. Eddington constructed his hypothesis long before developments in cognitive psychology and artificial intelligence resulted in specific knowledge of the operations of the human mind. These advances in cognitive science have impressed the eminent theoretical physicist Stephen Hawkins to further Eddington's hypothesis and turn it in the unexpected direction wherein computer programs rather than human minds create theoretical physics.

At present computers are a useful aid in research but they have to be directed by human minds. However, if one extrapolates their recent rapid rate of development, it would seem quite possible that they will take over altogether in theoretical physics. So maybe the end is in sight for theoretical physicists if not for theoretical physics [Hawkins, quoted in Davis and Hersh, 1986, p. 158].

Logical Implication and Production System

It is important to distinguish logical implication from the similarly appearing production system or production rule. Logical implication is concerned with propositions and their truth. A production rule is concerned with the action to be taken when conditions are met. In logical implication, the validity of deductive reasoning can be guaranteed if the rules of predicate logic are followed. In a production system, the actions taken when conditions are met may be practically useful or appropriate, but the executed procedure carries no guarantee. The symbolic expression or formula for a logical implication is: $P_1 \ldots P_n \subset Q$. In ordinary English, it is true that propositions $P_1 \ldots P_n$ imply proposition Q. The symbolic expression or formula for a production rule is $C_1 \ldots C_n > A$. The essential nature of a production rule is that it is a command so that $C > A$ is to be followed even when A is "conclude Q." Production rules have the character of imperative procedures in contrast to logical implication concerned with the truth or falsity of propositions.

Logical Implication and Turing's Theory of Computation

At the beginning of this section, I indicated the central place that logical implication has in my general unified theory of natural and artificial intelligence. Modern programming languages such as PROLOG are applications of the logic of implication (Kowalski, 1979). The truth functional character of logical implication constitutes the formal representation of the two most basic procedural operations of the Turing machine. I express the formal representation of these operations as (1) $P_0 \subset Q_1$, (2) $P_1 \subset Q_0$.

The Turing machine, an abstract computer (Turing, 1936), can be briefly described as follows:

A Turing machine consists of two primary (theoretical) units: a "tape drive" and a "computation unit." The tape drive has a tape of infinite length on which there can be written (and subsequently read) any series of two symbols: 0 (zero) and 1 (one). The computation unit contains a program that consists of a sequence of commands made up from the list of operations below. Each "command" consists of two specified operations, one to be followed if the last symbol read by the machine was a 0 and one if it has just read a 1. Below are the Turing machine operations:

   Read tape
   Move tape left
   Move tape right
   Write 0 on the tape
   Write 1 on the tape
   Jump to another command
   Halt

[Kurzweil, 1990, p. 112].

Computation Theory and Intelligence

Turing's mathematical proofs (1936) concerning the universal Turing machine that can simulate the performance of any conceivable computer, the existence of problems that can never be solved but which are known to possess unique solutions, and the existence of infinitely equal unsolvable problems and solvable problems must be sharply delineated from Turing's psychological conjecture (Turing, 1950) that the human brain and its intelligence are computationally tractable and subsumable under the mathematical theory of the universal Turing machine. Turing's proposal (1950) of "the imitation game" as a test of parity between computer intelligence and human intelligence is an inadequate criterion of his psychological conjecture whose limits must be tested by the usual procedures of science. The computability of the brain and its intelligence must stand or fall in the outcome of empirical inquiry into neural and cognitive processes.

Limits of Logic, Mathematics, and Theories of Intelligence

Systems of logic and mathematics have theoretical limits as proven by Turing (1936), Church (1956), and Gödel (1931). In sufficiently complex systems of logic and mathematics, there exist propositions that are definitely true or definitely false, but which of these two truth values is correct can never be established with certainty. These limits apply to theories of intelligence, both natural and artificial.

Logical Implication and Psychology of Reasoning

As a formal symbolic structure, logical implication is a regular constituent of computational intelligence and a staple of university courses in symbolic logic. In everyday reasoning, people regularly depend on the inferential strength of logical implication, but they do not reason their way through everyday problems by manipulating the predicate calculus symbols that represent logical implication (Wagman, 1978, 1984). Instead, they use pragmatic forms of implication (if, then) and ordinary language (Leahey and Wagman, 1974; Wagman, 1979, 1980). The symbols of logical implication, like the symbols of algebra, possess great generality because of their abstract character, but specific applications of the logic of implication or the mathematics of algebra will entail specific contexts and specific meanings. The psychological application of logical implication has been investigated by Cheng and Holyoak (1985), and their work has been summarized by Hunt (1989, p. 619) as follows:

Cheng and Holyoak (1985) brought the study of generalized reasoning schemas into the laboratory. They showed that the logical connective "implication" is, psychologically, represented by several different "pragmatic reasoning schemas." One is the permission schema: If A occurs then B is permitted (e.g. "If a traveler is inoculated, then the traveler may enter the country"). Another is obligation: If A has happened, then the actor must do B (e.g. "In order to use the library you must have a card"). Both schemas are examples of implication. Psychologically, however, the conditions indicating the applicability of causal and permission schemas are different.

Logical Implication: Gödel and Artificial Intelligence

Logical implication was central to Gödel's analytical proof of his famous mathematical theorems. Gödel's theorems, which place limits on the logical completeness and consistency of mathematical systems, have sometimes been interpreted as placing unique limits on artificial intelligence.

The equivalence of probability and logical implication was first proved by Gödel (Gödel, 1930); proofs appear in textbooks on logic. The incompleteness of any finite axiomatization of arithmetic also was proved by Gödel (Gödel, 1931). Although this result is extremely important in mathematical logic, it does not (as some people have claimed [Lucas, 1961]) *preclude the possibility that machines will be able to reason as well as people* [italics added]. People cannot prove consistency of complex systems in this way either! [Genesereth and Nilsson, 1987, p. 62].

Mathematical proofs have sometimes been used to demonstrate that there are limits to the powers of artificial intelligence, in general, and of computers in particular (Dreyfus, 1972). For example, Gödel's theorem (1931) demonstrates that for any sufficiently complex logical system, propositions can be stated that can neither be disproved nor proved within that system, without the system itself being logically inconsistent. However, the application of Gödel's theorem to demonstrate theoretical limits of computers equally extends to demonstrate theoretical limits to the powers of human intelligence. In any case, Gödel's theorem has not impeded advances in the field of mathematics, nor should it impede advances in the field of artificial intelligence [Wagman, 1988, p. 11].

Production Rules as Theoretical Constructs

In cognitive psychology and artificial intelligence, production rules are theoretical variables that control the representation and processing of information or knowledge. The role of production rules in the human information processing system and their distinction from the stimulus-response variables or behaviors are set forth in accounts by Newell (1990) and Anderson (1983).

Logical Implication: Production System and Representation in Artificial Intelligence

The general unified theory of intelligence describes the concept of production system as an implementation of logical implication. In turn, the production system concept is fundamental in artificial intelligence in that the many distinct methods of knowledge representation in artificial intelligence can all be reduced to the theory of production systems.

A production system consists of:

A set of rules, each consisting of a left side (a pattern) that determines the applicability of the rule and a right side that describes the operation to be performed if the rule is applied.

One or more knowledge/databases that contain whatever information is appropriate for the particular task. Some parts of the database may be permanent, while other parts of it may pertain only to the solution of the current problem. *The information in these databases may be structured in any appropriate way* [italics added] [Rich and Knight, 1991, p. 36].

Post (1943) provided a mathematical demonstration that any representational formalism in artificial intelligence can be subsumed under the theory of the production system (Wagman, 1991b, p. 62).

Logical Implication: The Resolution Method in Artificial Intelligence

Logical implication in the form of a *reductio ad absurdum* argument is important in the classic artificial intelligence method of resolution.

In a way we may regard Euclid's method of proof as foreshadowing the development of the general resolution theory of theorem-proving in artificial intelligence (Robinson, 1965). Thus, Euclid's use of the logical deduction law *reductio ad absurdum* to prove that the square root of two is an irrational number . . . is echoed in Robinson's use of *reductio ad absurdum* as the central logical mechanism by which the general resolution method in artificial intelligence accomplishes the goal of mathematical theorem-proving and general problem solving (Cheng and Juang, 1987; Genesereth, 1983).

The powerful mathematical reasoning method of *reductio ad absurdum*, as used by many creative mathematicians (including Alan Turing) to establish the proof of a proposition or theorem, consists of a sequential logical procedure. The sequence begins with the assumption that the proposition or theorem is false, continues with mathematical deductions that follow from the initial assumption, and concludes with a demonstration that these deductions culminate in the contradiction of the initial assumption that the proposition or theorem was false.

Resolution is used to prove theorems that are written in the predicate calculus (Chang and Lee, 1973). The predicate calculus, in turn, represents a state of affairs or problem state. Proving the theorem becomes equivalent to problem solving.

Contradiction or refutation is the goal in theorem-proving by the general resolution method. Contradiction or refutation proves the falsity of the negation of a proposition and thus establishes its truth.

The general strategy of resolution in a theorem-proving system involves a set of procedures that begins with the representation of a state of affairs in the language of the predicate calculus. . . . The predicate calculus expressions are rewritten as groupings of logic symbols, termed clauses. . . . The inference rules of resolution are then applied to the clauses.

These inference rules are directed toward a gradual simplification of the set of clauses (in large systems, thousands of clauses may be involved; Clocksin and Mellish, 1981). Simplification involves the conversion, by means of rules of logic . . . of conjunctions into disjunctions and implications into disjunctions. Resolution is then applied to disjunctive clauses that are complementary in sign. These pairs of clauses are then resolved, that is, eliminated from the set of clauses. The process continues with the elimination of further clauses until the nil . . . or empty clause is produced (no complementary disjunctions remain).

The resolution method is designed to enable computer systems to solve problems by theorem-proving. The logic of the theorem-proving and the resolution by refutation or contradiction can be briefly summarized.

From a set of propositions, prove some goal X. The first step is to negate the goal X. The second step is to add the negation of X to the set of propositions, thus forming an expanded set. The third step is to transform the expanded set of propositions into a set of clauses (groupings of predicate calculus expressions).

The fourth step is to apply resolution to the set of clauses with the intended purpose of deriving a contradiction (the nil clause). From the contradiction, the final logical step is the negation of the negation of the goal X; that is, the proof of the theorem is established [Wagman, 1991b, pp. 41–46].

The Formal Core of Types of Implication Statements

Implication statements may be of different types, but they have a formal core. The formal core abstracts the essence of the relationship between the antecedent and the consequent parts of the implication statement. As an abstraction, the formal core ignores some of the distinctive meaning of the type of implication. The valid formal core of an implication statement requires that it is not the case that both the antecedent is true and the consequent is false. Types of implication statements include logical conditionals, definitional conditionals, causal conditionals, and decisional conditionals. Conditionals are ordinarily expressed as if-then statements, and their content is indefinitely varied, but their formal validity is singularly determined by the criterion stated earlier.

Logical Form versus Psychological Content

The nature of logic is often misunderstood by research psychologists. The misunderstanding centers around three characteristics of logic that separate it as a discipline from psychology. First, logic is concerned with validity of argument, not with truth or content of the argument. Second, logic is abstract and formal in that it is concerned with variables and rules of inference, not with psychological behavior and everyday reasoning. Third, logic is concerned only with the minimum condition necessary to establish validity, not with the many conditions, contexts, and contents of psychological experience and behavior.

The Use of Abstract Rules in Human Reasoning

A central issue in comparing human and artificial reasoning concerns the importance of abstract rules of inference. Clearly, insofar as artificial intelligence employs a predicate calculus, its reasoning is abstract. It is also the case that logicians and mathematicians in their formal professional work use systems of deductive inference. However, do they, and people in general, employ abstract rules in everyday reasoning and problem solving? This important question was addressed by Smith, Langston, and Nisbett (1992, p. 1).

A number of theoretical positions in psychology — including variants of case-based reasoning, instance-based analogy, and connectionist models — maintain that abstract rules are not involved in human reasoning, or at best play a minor role. Other views hold that the use of abstract rules is a core aspect of human reasoning. We propose eight criteria for determining whether or not people use abstract rules in reasoning, and examine evidence relevant to each criterion for several rule systems. We argue that there is substantial evidence that several different inferential rules, including modus ponens, contractual rules, causal rules, and the law of large numbers, are used in solving everyday problems. We discuss the implications for various theoretical positions and consider hybrid mechanisms that combine aspects of instance and rule models.

The General Theory and Symbolic-Connectionist Paradigms

A general unified theory of intelligence would need to be inclusive of a dual typology of human cognition and a dual typology of computational models. Deliberative human thought, as represented by reasoning, problem solving, planning, judgment, and decision making, is distinguished from automatic human memory, as represented by retrieval and recognition processes. The first set of cognitive activities is best modeled by symbolic computational models, the second by connectionist computational models. A complete account of cognition will require an integration of the symbolic and connectionist architectures. In the general unified theory of intelligence, both the cognition and the models have their ultimate foundation in the logic of implication.

Holyoak and Spellman (1993) provide a useful account of integrated symbolic-connectionist architectures.

The fact that human cognition has both symbolic and subsymbolic aspects encourages various attempts to integrate the approaches. A number of suggestions for hybrid "symbolic-connectionist" models have been offered (e.g., Dyer, 1991; Holyoak, 1991; Minsky, 1991). These models can be divided roughly into two classes. One class of models maintains a core of "traditional" symbolic machinery (e.g., discrete propositions and rules) to represent relation structures, while adding connectionist-style mechanisms for "soft" constraint satisfaction. The second class of models seeks to develop connectionist representations of relation structures by introducing techniques for handling the binding of objects to roles. We review examples of each of these approaches to integrating the two theoretical perspectives.

Soft Constraint Satisfaction in Reasoning

The generation and evaluation of beliefs — the central task of induction — has a holistic quality that has posed grave difficulty for theoretical treatments. Tweney (1990) identified the complex interrelatedness of hypotheses as a major challenge for computational theories of scientific reasoning. Fodor (1983) has taken the pessimistic position that little progress is to be expected in understanding central cognition because the facts relevant to any belief cannot be circumscribed (i.e., we do not operate within a closed world) and the degree of confirmation of any hypothesis is sensitive to properties of the whole system of beliefs. As Quine (1961, p. 41) put it, "our statements about the external world face the tribunal of sense experience not individually but only as a corporate body." A psychological theory of induction must identify mechanisms that can cope with the holistic quality of hypothesis evaluation (Holland et al., 1986).

One mechanism with the requisite properties is parallel constraint satisfaction, a basic capability of connectionist models. In a connectionist network, local computations involving individual units interact to generate stable global patterns of activity over the entire network. Models that perform "soft" constraint satisfaction over units corresponding to relation structures can attempt to capitalize on the complementary strengths of symbolic representation and connectionist processing. Such symbolic-connectionist models can make inferences based on incomplete information, which standard symbolic systems are often unable to do, using knowledge that distributed connectionist systems cannot readily represent. Models of this sort have been used to account for psychological data concerning text comprehension, analogical reasoning, and evaluation of explanations.

Kintsch (1988) has developed a symbolic-connectionist model to deal with the resolution of ambiguities during text comprehension. His "construction-integration" model has four main components: 1. initial parallel activation of memory concepts corresponding to words in the text, together with formation of propositions by parsing rules; 2. spreading of activation to a small number of close associates of the text concepts; 3. inferring additional propositions by inference rules; and 4. creating excitatory and inhibitory links, with associated weights, between units representing activated concepts and propositions, and allowing the network to settle. The entire process is iterative. A small portion of text is processed, the units active after the settling process are maintained, and then the cycle is repeated with the next portion of text. In addition to accounting for psycholinguistic data on text comprehension, the construction-integration model has been extended to simulate levels of expertise in planning routine computing tasks (Mannes & Kintsch, 1991).

Symbolic-connectionist models have been developed to account for two of the basic processes in analogical reasoning — retrieving useful analogs from memory and mapping the elements of a known situation (the source analog) and a new situation (the target analog) to identify useful correspondences. Because analogical mapping requires finding correspondences on the basis of relation structure, most distributed connectionist models lack the requisite representational tools to do it. Purely symbolic models have difficulty avoiding combinatorial explosion when searching for possible analogs in a large memory store and when searching for optimal mappings between two analogs. The two symbolic-connectionist models — the ACME model of Holyoak and Thagard (1989), which does analogical mapping, and the ARCS model of Thagard et al. (1990), which does analogical retrieval — operate by taking symbolic, predicate-calculus-style representations of situations as inputs, applying a small set of abstract constraints to build a network of units representing possible mappings between elements of two analogs, and then allowing parallel constraint satisfaction to settle the network into a stable state in which asymptotic activations of units reflect degree of confidence in possible mappings. The constraints on mapping lead to preferences for sets of mapping hypotheses that yield isomorphic correspondences, link similar elements, and map elements of special importance. These same constraints (with differing relative impacts) operate in both the mapping and retrieval models. The mapping model has been applied successfully to model human judgments about complex naturalistic analogies (Spellman & Holyoak, 1992) and has been extended to account for data concerning analogical transfer in mathematical problem solving (Holyoak, Novick, and Melz, 1993).

Thagard (1989, 1992) has shown that the problem of evaluating competing explanations can be addressed by a symbolic-connectionist model of explanatory coherence, ECHO. The model takes as inputs symbolic representations of basic explanatory relations between propositions corresponding to data and explanatory hypotheses. The system then builds a constraint network linking units representing the propositions, using a small number of very general constraints that support explanations with greater explanatory breadth (more links to data), greater simplicity (fewer constituent assumptions), and greater correspondence to analogous explanations of other phenomena. Relations of mutual coherence (modeled by symmetrical excitatory links) hold between hypotheses and the data they explain; relations of competition (inhibitory links) hold between rival hypotheses. Parallel constraint satisfaction settles the network into an asymptotic state in which units representing the most mutually coherent hypotheses and data are active and units representing inconsistent rivals are deactivated. Thagard (1989) showed that ECHO can model a number of realistic cases of explanation evaluation in both scientific and legal contexts; Schank & Ranney (1991, 1992; Ranney, 1993) have used the model to account for students' belief revision in the context of physics problems; and Read & Marcus-Newhall (1993) have applied the model to the evaluation of explanations of everyday events.

Reflexive Reasoning Using Dynamic Binding
Whereas the models discussed above involve various hybridizations of connectionist processing mechanisms and symbolic representations, a second class of models attempts to provide pure connectionist-style representations of complex relational knowledge. . . . Shastri & Ajjangadde (1993) have developed a detailed computational model that use temporal dynamics to code the relation structure of propositions and rules. Dynamic bindings in working memory are represented by units firing in phase. Consider a proposition such as "John gave the book to Mary." On a single phase, the unit representing the object John will fire in synchrony with a unit representing the "giver" role; in a different phase the unit for Mary will fie in synchrony with a unit for the "recipient" role. The system is object-based, in the sense that each time slice is occupied by the firing of a single active object unit together with units for all the argument roles that the object fills. Bindings are systematically propagated to make inferences by means of links between units for argument slots. For example, in a rule stating that "If someone receives something, then they own it," the "recipient" role in the antecedent of the rule will be connected to the "owner" role in the consequent. Accordingly, if Mary is dynamically bound to the "recipient" role (by phase locking firing of the "Mary" and "recipient" units), then Mary will become bound to the "owner" role as well (i.e., the unit for Mary will fire in phase with units for *both* relevant roles). Shastri & Ajjangadde show that their model can answer questions based on inference rules in time that is linear with the length of the inference chain but independent of the number of rules in memory — the most efficient performance pattern theoretically possible.

Shastri & Ajjangadde (1993) note a number of interesting psychological implications of their dynamic binding model. In particular, they distinguish between two forms of reasoning, which they term "reflexive" and "reflective." Reflexive reasoning is based on spontaneous and efficient inferences drawn in the course of everyday understanding, whereas reflective reasoning is the deliberate and effortful deliberation required in conscious planning and problem solving. It is intriguing that humans are far better at text comprehension than, for example, syllogistic reasoning, even though the formal logical complexity of the former task is much greater than that of the latter (Stenning & Oaksford, 1993). In terms of the Shastri & Ajjangadde model, text comprehension mainly involves reflexive reasoning, whereas syllogistic inference requires reflective reasoning. Fluent comprehension draws upon a rich network of stored rules, which are used in conjunction with the input to establish a coherent, elaborated model of the situation. Reflexive reasoning of the sort involved in ordinary comprehension relies on dynamic binding of objects to argument slots in preexisting rules. These rules have been encoded into long-term memory, with appropriate interconnections between their arguments. In contrast, reflective reasoning requires manipulation of knowledge in absence of relevant prestored rules. An arbitrary deductive syllogism (e.g., "If all artists are beekeepers, and some beekeepers are chemists, what follows?") is unrelated to any store rules; rather, understanding the premises requires setting up de novo "rules" (e.g., "If someone is an artist, then that person is a beekeeper") for each problem.

Shastri & Ajjangadde's model predicts that reflexive reasoning will be constrained by limits on the number of multiply-instantiated predicates, as well as by patterns of variable repetition across the arguments of a rule. The model also makes predictions about the limits of the information that can be active simultaneously in working memory. Although the number of active argument units is potentially unlimited, the number of objects that can be reasoned about in a single session is limited to the number of distinct phases available (because only one object unit may fire in a single phase). Given plausible assumptions about the speed of neural activity, this limit on the number of active objects can be calculated as being five or fewer. This figure is strikingly similar to Miller's (1956) estimate of short-term memory capacity and is consistent with work by Halford & Wilson (1980) indicating that adults cannot simultaneously represent relations involving more than four elements. For example, recent empirical evidence (described by Halford et al., 1993) confirms a limit that will be recognized by anyone who has worked with statistical interactions: The most complex statistical relation that people can deal with in working memory is a 3-way interaction (which involves three independent variables and one dependent variable, for a total of four dimensions). Experimental studies of people's memory for bindings between individuals and properties have revealed similar capacity limits, as well as error patterns consistent with distributed representations of bindings (Stenning & Levy, 1988; Stenning et al., 1988). Recent work has extended the temporal-synchrony approach to other forms of reasoning. Hummel & Holyoak (1992) have shown that the principles embodied in Holyoak & Thagard's (1989) ACME model of analogical mapping can be captured by a model that encodes propositional structure by temporal synchrony.

An interesting feature of the synchrony approach is that the need to minimize "cross talk" between the constituents of relation structures encourages postulating specific types of serial processing at the "micro" level of temporal phases. For example, in the Shastri & Ajjangadde model only one object is allowed to fire in each time slice. It is also noteworthy that their model combines localist representations of concepts with distributed control and, thus, exemplifies a theoretical "middle ground" between traditional production system and fully distributed connectionist networks. It is possible that attempts to develop connectionist models of symbol systems will cast new light on the limits of parallel information processing. In addition, connectionist models may provide more effective implementations of the flexible recognition processes based on long-term memory that appear crucial to expertise (Chase & Simon, 1973). More generally, the confluence of the symbolic and connectionist paradigms seems likely to deepen our understanding of the kinds of computations that constitute human thinking. (Holyoak & Spellman, 1993, pp. 272–277)

CRITIQUES OF PURE REASON

The Ultimate Nature of Cognition

Philosophical approaches to the ultimate nature of cognition have their preeminent source in the works of Plato (1956) and derivative advances in the works of Descartes (1951), Hobbes (1651), Locke (1975), and Kant (1958).

Plato believed in a world of ideas beyond sense perception. Plato's world possessed ultimate truth, absolute certainty, and undisturbed permanence. This pristine and abstract world could be approached by the study of mathematics, because its truths were permanent, certain, and universal. The Platonic faith in the absolute truth and purity of mathematical reason dominated the later philosophical thought of Descartes, Hobbes, Locke, and Kant, for whom Euclidean geometry possessed a body of truth and a method of reasoning that constituted a bulwark against error and an unassailable paragon of philosophical investigation into the nature of cognition.

Descartes agreed with Plato that mathematics was the key to understanding the universe, itself a colossal mathematical machine. Scrupulous deductive reasoning like that in Euclidean mathematics would disclose the laws of the universe.

Hobbes, like Plato, affirmed that mathematics and only mathematics reveals true knowledge of reality. All knowledge, except mathematical knowledge, is imperfect.

Locke, impressed with the power of mathematics displayed in the Newtonian description of the physical world, was convinced that the human mind was part of physical nature and could be accounted for in mathematical terms. The human mind creates propositions about reality, and the truth of these propositions can be determined by systematically comparing them for consistency or contradiction.

Kant's philosophy of cognition posited pure categories of space and time. These categories were innate, embedded in the brain's structure, independent of personal experience, and provided formal dimensions in which all empirical knowledge was bound and constrained. The pure categories of rationality provide the necessary conditions for logical thought and are normative for human reasoning. The pure categories of space, time, and formal logic are a priori templates into which all cognition is fitted.

We can say with confidence that certain pure a priori synthetical cognitions, pure mathematics and pure physics, are actual and given; for both contain propositions which are thoroughly recognized as absolutely certain . . . and yet as independent of experience [Kant, 1781].

Our intellect does not draw its laws from nature but imposes its laws on nature [Kant, 1781].

The linchpin in Kant's universally admired philosophy was his deep belief that Euclidean geometry was not derived from experience but, rather, was an a priori intuition regarding the true nature of physical space. Kant's philosophical edifice was devastated by the development of non-Euclidean geometries that lead to curious theorems, at variance with Euclidean theorems but appropriate to the description of many types of physical space for which the Euclidean system was inapplicable or inadequate. Kant's confident assertion that Euclidean geometry was an a priori truth and the only true empirical geometry collapsed following Riemann's (1953) development of differential geometry. Riemann demonstrated that Euclidean geometry was only a special case derivable from a general equation whose variables and functions could embrace a very large set of possible geometries applicable to possible sets of physical space.

Artificial Intelligence and Naive Physics

Logical approaches to artificial intelligence have demonstrated the power of axioms and deductive systems in the domains of scientific and mathematical reasoning, but the domain of commonsense reasoning contains formidable difficulties in that people do not employ theoretical knowledge of physics or psychology in their everyday reasoning about the physical or social world. Yet, people appear to have a satisfactory working knowledge of events and processes in the physical world, and according to Turing's thesis (Turing, 1963), this knowledge does fall under the aegis of computational logic. The Turing thesis has been supported by the work of Hayes (1985), who has demonstrated that everyday concepts embedded in naive physics and naive psychology can be stated in the predicate calculus and can be expressed as logical theorems that lead to true or false deductive inferences. This axiomatization includes people's commonsense knowledge and reasoning concerning cause and effect, velocity and acceleration, weight and balance, height and support, path and boundary, and inside and outside.

Artificial Intelligence and Logicism

The logicism of the Hayes research program has been criticized by McDermott (1990) on the grounds that pure deductive reasoning as a set of formal axioms is not applicable to human thinking, which is largely nondeductive. McDermott (1990) points out that human reasoning is typically nonmonotonic, that it easily takes account of changes in premises, context, and conditions, whereas the monotonic logicism of axiomatic deduction is rigid. McDermott concludes that only when the logicism approach can be extended to cover nonmonotonic everyday thinking will a valid science of intelligence be possible, and pending that development, only an applied technology of computer programs that do makeshift nondeductive reasoning will persist.

To summarize: the logicist project of expressing "naive physics" in first-order logic has not been very successful. One reason may be that the basic argument was flawed. You cannot write down axioms independent of a program for manipulating them if the inferences you are interested in are not deductions. Unfortunately, very few interesting inferences are deductions, and the attempts by logicists to extend logic to cover more territory have been disappointing. Hence we must resign ourselves to writing programs, and viewing knowledge representations as entities to be manipulated by the programs [McDermott, quoted in Boden, 1990, p. 227].

Conclusion

Mathematics and mathematical logic have been largely responsible for advances in the physical sciences. Whether mathematical logic can serve an analogous role in the development of the sciences of cognition remains to be seen. It may be that nonstandard forms of mathematical logic will have to be created to capture human thinking, which is more often finesse than ratiocination: "Life is the art of drawing sufficient conclusions from insufficient premises" (Butler, quoted in Kline, 1985, p. 210).

ARTIFICIAL INTELLIGENCE AND ITS OBJECTIVES

The field of artificial intelligence, a specialized discipline within general computer science, is directed toward the continuous augmentation of computer intelligence. The augmentation of intelligence in computers may be achieved by two general methods or by a combination of the methods.

In the first general method, the computer models the cognitive processes of human intellect. Augmentation of computer intelligence through this method requires the continuous expansion of reliable and valid knowledge concerning human cognitive processes.

In the second general method, the intelligence of the computer models formal logical structures and processes. Augmentation of computer intelligence through this method requires the continuous expansion of reliable and valid knowledge concerning the theory and application of systems of logic and coordinated sets of programming languages.

These two general methods of augmenting computer intelligence depend for their physical realization on the continuous expansion of knowledge in the field of computer engineering. Improvements in computer engineering design and materials (for example, from serial to parallel processing, from electronic to optical circuitry) optimize the results of the application of the two general methods of artificial intelligence.

In addition to the engineering objective of the augmentation of the intelligence of computers, the field of artificial intelligence also has a scientific objective concerned with the development of a general theory of intelligence. This abstract science of intelligence would systematically establish the general principles, commonalities, and singularities of human, animal, and computer intelligence.

FOUNDATIONAL PROBLEMS OF ARTIFICIAL INTELLIGENCE

As is true of any science, it is important to inquire into the conceptual foundations of artificial intelligence. Kirsh (1991) provides a critical inquiry into the foundational assumptions of artificial intelligence.

The Foundational Assumptions of Artificial Intelligence: Overview

Kirsh (1991) has identified five far-reaching general assumptions that lie at the foundations of artificial intelligence research. In the following section, these assumptions and the theoretical positions taken on them by various research programs are discussed.

The objective of research in the foundations of AI [artificial intelligence] is to address . . . basic questions of method, theory, and orientation. It is to self-consciously reappraise what AI is all about.

The pursuit of AI does not occur in isolation. Fields such as philosophy, linguistics, psychophysics and theoretical computer science have exercised a historical influence over the field and today there is as much dialogue as ever, particularly with the new field of cognitive science. One consequence of dialogue is that criticisms of positions held in one discipline frequently apply to positions held in other disciplines.

In this . . . essay, my objective is to bring together a variety of these arguments both for and against the dominant research programs of AI.

It is impossible, of course, to explore carefully all of these arguments in a single paper. . . . *It may be of use, though, to stand back and consider several of the most abstract assumptions underlying the competing visions of intelligence. These assumptions — whether explicitly named by theorists or not — identify issues which have become focal points of debate and serve as dividing lines of positions.*

Of these, five stand out as particularly fundamental:

— *Pre-eminence of knowledge and conceptualization: Intelligence that transcends insect-level intelligence requires declarative knowledge and some form of reasoning-like computation — call this cognition. Core AI is the study of the conceptualizations of the world presupposed and used by intelligent systems during cognition.*
— *Disembodiment: Cognition and the knowledge it presupposes can be studied largely in abstraction from the details of perception and motor control.*

— *Kinematics of cognition are language-like: It is possible to describe the trajectory of knowledge states or informational states created during cognition using a vocabulary very much like English or some regimented logicomathematical version of English.*
— *Learning can be added later: The kinematics of cognition and the domain knowledge needed for cognition can be studied separately from the study of concept learning, psychological development, and evolutionary change.*
— *Uniform architecture: There is a single architecture underlying virtually all cognition.*

Different research programs are based, more or less, on an admixture of these assumptions plus corollaries.

Logicism (Hobbs & Moore, 1985; Newel & Simon, 1972) as typified by formal theorists of the commonsense world, formal theorists of language and formal theorists of belief (Konolize, 1985; Levesque, 1986), presupposes almost all of these assumptions. Logicism, as we know it today, is predicated on the preeminence of reasoning-like processes and conceptualization, the legitimacy of disembodied analysis, on interpreting rational kinematics as propositional, and the possibility of separating thought and learning. It remains neutral on the uniformity of the underlying architecture.

Other research programs make a virtue of denying one or more of these assumptions. SOAR (Newell, 1990; Rosenbloom et al., 1991), for instance, differs from logicism in according learning a vital role in the basic theory and in assuming that all of cognition can be explained as processes occurring in a single uniform architecture. Rational kinematics in SOAR are virtually propositional but differ slightly in containing control markers — preferences — to bias transitions. In other respects, SOAR shares with logicism the assumption that reasoning-like processes and conceptualization are central, and that it is methodologically acceptable to treat central processes in abstraction from perceptual and motor processes.

Connectionists (McClelland, Rumelhart, & the PDP Research Group, 1986; Rumelhart, McClelland, & the PDP Research Group, 1986), by contrast, deny that reasoning-like processes are preeminent in cognition, that core AI is the study of the concepts underpinning domain understanding, and that rational kinematics is language-like. Yet like SOAR, connectionists emphasize the centrality of learning in the study of cognition, and like logicists they remain agnostic about the uniformity of the underlying architecture. They are divided on the assumption of disembodiment.

Roboticists (Brooks, 1991) take the most extreme stance and deny reasoning, conceptualization, rational kinematics, disembodiment, uniformity of architecture and the separability of knowledge and learning (more precisely evolution). Part of what is attractive in the robotics approach is precisely its radicalness.

Similar profiles can be offered for Lenat and Feigenbaum's position (1991), Minsky's society of mind theory (1986), Schank's antiformalist approach (1985; with Riesbeck, 1981) and Hewitt (1991) and Gasser's (1991) account of much of distributed AI research [italics added] [Kirsch, 1991, pp. 3–5].

In order to facilitate comparisons of theoretical positions of various research programs on the foundational assumptions discussed by Kirsh (1991, pp. 3–4), I have constructed Table 1.1, which indicates the position (denied, affirmed, neutral) of each of four research programs/theories (logicism, connectionism, SOAR, roboticism) on each of the five assumptions.

TABLE 1.1

Comparison of Theoretical Positions of Logicism, Connectionism, SOAR, and Roboticism on Foundational Assumptions in Artificial Intelligence

	Theoretical Positions			
Assumptions	*Logicism[a]*	*Connectionism[b]*	*SOAR[c]*	*Roboticism[d]*
The Essentiality of Knowledge, Conceptualization, and Reasoning-like Computation Processes	Affirmed	Denied	Affirmed	Denied
The Separateness of Cognition from Perceptual-Motor Processes	Affirmed	Divided	Affirmed	Denied
The Adequacy of English or Symbolic Languages to Describe Cognition	Affirmed	Denied	Affirmed	Denied
The Separateness of Cognition from Learning	Affirmed	Denied	Denied	Denied
The Uniformity of Cognitive Architecture	Neutral	Neutral	Affirmed	Denied

Note: The indicated theoretical positions are general and modal.
[a]From Hobbs & Moore, 1985; Newell & Simon, 1972.
[b]From McClelland, Rumelhart, & the PDP Research Group, 1986; Rumelhart, McClelland, & the PDP Research Group, 1986.
[c]From Newell, 1990; Rosenbloom et al., 1991.
[d]From Brooks, 1991.
Source: Based on Kirsh, D. (1991). Foundations of AI: The big issues. *Artificial Intelligence, 47*, 3–30.

First Assumption: Essentiality of Knowledge, Conceptualization, and Reasoning-Like Computation

In general, artificial intelligence theorists and researchers (with the exception of roboticists and connectionists) agree on the economical necessity of knowledge and inference. Knowledge can be declarative or compiled, and inference can be explicit or implicit.

In accepting the priority of knowledge level theories, one is not committed to supposing that knowledge is explicitly encoded declaratively and deployed in explicitly inferential processes, although frequently knowledge will be. One's commitment is that knowledge and conceptualization lie at the heart of AI: that a major goal in the field is to discover the basic knowledge units of cognition (or intelligent skills).

What are these knowledge units? In the case of qualitative theories of the commonsense world, and in the case of Lenat's CYC project (Lenat & Guha, 1989; Lenat & Feigenbaum, 1991), these basic knowledge units are the conceptual units of *consensus reality* — the core concepts underpinning "the millions of things that we all know and that we assume everyone else knows" (Lenat & Guha, 1989, p. 4). Not surprisingly, these concepts are often familiar ideas with familiar names — though sometimes they will be theoretical ideas, having a technical meaning internal to the theory.

The basic idea that knowledge and conceptualization lie at the heart of AI stems from the seductive view that cognition is inference. Intelligent skills, an old truism of AI runs, are composed of two parts: a declarative knowledge base and an inference engine.

The inference engine is relatively uncomplicated; it is a domain-independent program that takes as input a set of statements about the current situation plus a fragment of the declarative knowledge base; it produces as output a stream of inferred declaratives culminating in the case of decision making and routine activity, in directives for appropriate action.

In contrast to the inference engine, the knowledge base is domain-specific and is as complicated as a cognitive skill requires. Domain knowledge is what distinguishes the ability to troubleshoot a circuit from the ability to understand the meaning of a sentence. Both require knowledge but of different domains. It follows that the heart of the AI problem is to discover what the agent knows about the world that permits success. This idea, *in one form or another*, has been endorsed by logicists, by Lenat and Feigenbaum (1991), Chomsky (1956), Montague (1974), and, with variations, by Schank and Riesbeck (1981), and Newell and Simon (1972).

The qualification *in one form or another* is significant. As mentioned, a commitment to theorizing about knowledge and knowledge units is not in itself a commitment to large amounts of on-line logical reasoning or explicit representation of domain knowledge. It is well known that not all skills that require intelligent control require an *explicit* knowledge base. So it is a further thesis that declarative knowledge and logical inference are actually deployed in most cognitive skills. In such cases we still may say that cognition is inference, but we no longer expect to find explicit inference rules or even complete trajectories of inferential steps. In the source code of cognition we would find instructions for inferential processes throughout. But knowledge can be compiled into procedures or designed into control systems which have no distinct inference engines. So often our account of cognition is more of the form "The system is acting *as if* it were inferring. . . ."

Knowledge compilation One question of considerable interest among theorists who accept the centrality of knowledge and the virtue of knowledge level theories, is "How far can this knowledge compilation go?"

According to Nilsson there are severe limits on this compilation. Overt declaratives have special virtues.

> The most versatile intelligent machines will represent much of their knowledge about their environment declaratively. . . . [A declarative can] be used by the machine even for purposes unforeseen by the machine's designer, it [can] more easily be modified than could knowledge embodied in programs, and it facilitate[s] communication between the machine and other machines and humans [Nilsson, 1991].

For Nilsson, the theory of what is known is a good approximation of what is actually represented declaratively. He suggests that some reactions to situations and some useful inferences may be compiled. But storage and indexing cost militate against compiling knowledge overmuch. Real flexibility requires explicit declarative representation of knowledge. No doubt, it is an empirical question as to just how much of a cognitive skill can be compiled. But as long as a system uses some explicit declaratives, the apparatus of declarative representation must be in place, making it possible, when time permits, to control action through run time interference.

Rosenschein and Kaebling (1986) see the inflexibility of knowledge compilation as far less constraining. On their view, a significant range of tasks connected with adaptive response to the environment can be compiled. To determine the appropriate set of reactions to build into a machine, a designer performs the relevant knowledge level of logical reasoning at compile time so that the results will be available at run time. Again, it is an empirical matter how many cognitive skills can be completely automatized in this fashion. But the research program of situated automata is to push the envelope as far as possible.

A similar line of thought applies to the work of Chomsky and Montague. When they claim to be offering a theory about the knowledge deployed in parsing and speech production it does not follow they require on-line inference. By offering their theories in the format of "here's the knowledge base use the obvious inference engine" they establish the effectiveness of their knowledge specification: it is a condition on their theory that when conjoined with the obvious inference engine it should generate all and only syntactic strings (or some specified fragment of that set). That is why their theories are called *generative*. But to date no one has offered a satisfactory account of how the theory is to be effectively implemented. Parsing *may* involve considerable inference, but equally it may consist of highly automated retrieval processes where structures or fragments of structures previously found acceptable are recognized. To be sure, some theorists say that recognition in itself is a type of inference: that recognizing a string of words *as* a noun phrase (NP) involves inference. Hence even parsing construed as constraint satisfaction or as schema retrieval (instantiation) and so forth, is itself inferential at bottom. But this is not the dominant view. Whatever the answer, though, there are no *a priori* grounds for assuming that statements of linguistic principle are encoded explicitly in declaratives and operated on by explicit inference rules.

Whether knowledge be explicit or compiled, the view that cognition is inference and that theorizing at the knowledge level is at least the starting place of scientific AI is endorsed by a large fragment of the community [italics added].

Opposition In stark contrast is the position held by Rod Brooks. According to Brooks (1991) a theory in AI is not an account of the knowledge units of cognition. Most tasks that seem to involve considerable world knowledge may yet be achievable without appeal to declaratives, to concepts, or to basic knowledge units, even at compile time. Knowledge level theories, he argues, too often chase fictions. If AI's overarching goal is to understand intelligent control of action, then if it turns out to be true, as Brooks believes it will, that most intelligent behavior can be produced by a system of carefully tuned control systems interconnected in a simple but often ad hoc manner, then why study knowledge? A methodology more like experimental engineering is what is required.

If Brooks is right, intelligent control systems can be designed before a designer has an articulated conceptualization of the task environment. Moreover, the system itself can succeed without operating on a conceptualization in any interesting sense. New behaviors can be grown onto older behaviors in an evolutionary fashion that makes otiose the task of conceptualizing the world. The result is a system that, for a large class of tasks, might match the versatility of action achievable with declaratives, yet it never calls on the type of capacities we associate with having knowledge of a conceptualization and symbolic representation of the basic world elements [Kirsh, 1991, pp. 6–9].

The Second Assumption: The Separateness of Cognition from Perceptual-Motor Processes

The distinction between formal knowledge level theories and perceptual-motor theories is a distinction that belongs to the context of the designer of systems. The distinction does not belong to the system except where the system is a human system and a separation arises because conscious knowledge and symbolization is separated from neural structures that automatically accomplish perceptual motor action and the adaptation of the system to the environment. The distinction between the conscious knowledge level and the mnemonic knowledge level, between cognitive processes and sensory-motor processes, will gradually fade as research discloses more and more about the details of neural structures and functions that support both types of knowledge and of their interrelationships. The viewpoint I have just expressed is in contrast to the viewpoint taken by Kirsh (1991), as well as that of Brooks (1991) on robotic systems and those of Gibson (1979) on animal and human systems. The views of these theorists, together with those of Kirsh, are included in the following section.

I have been presenting a justification for the view that, in the main, intelligence can be fruitfully studied on the assumption that the problems and tasks facing intelligent agents can be formally specified and, so, pursued abstractly at the knowledge or conceptual level. For analytic purposes, we can ask questions about cognitive skills using symbolic characterizations of the environment as input and symbolic characterizations of motor activity as output. Concerns about how conceptual knowledge is *grounded* in perceptual-motor skills can be addressed separately. These questions can be bracketed because what differentiates cognitive skills is not so much the perceptual-motor parameters of a task but the knowledge of the task domain that directs action in that domain. This is the methodological assumption of disembodiment. What are the arguments against it?

In his attack on core artificial intelligence, Brooks (1991) identifies three assumptions related to disembodiment that, in his opinion, dangerously bias the way cognitive skills are studied:

The output of vision is conceptualized and, so, the interface between perception and "central cognition" is clean and neatly characterizable in the language of the predicate calculus or some other language with terms denoting objects and terms denoting properties.

Whenever we exercise our intelligence, we call on a central representation of the world state where some substantial fraction of the world state is represented and regularly updated perceptually or by inference.

When we seem to be pursuing our tasks in an organized fashion, our actions have been planned in advance by envisioning outcomes and choosing a sequence that best achieves the agent's goals.

The error in each of these assumptions, Brooks (1991) contends, is to suppose that the real world is somehow simple enough, sufficiently decomposable into concept-sized bites, that we can represent it, in real time, in all the detailed respects that might matter to achieving our goals. It is not. Even if we had enough concepts to cover its relevant aspects, we would never be able to compute an updated world model in real time. Moreover, we do not need to. Real success in a causally dense world is achieved by tuning the perceptual system to *action-relevant* changes.

To take an example from Gibson (1979), an earlier theorist who held similar views, if a creature's goals are to avoid obstacles on its path to a target, it is not necessary for it to constantly judge its distance from obstacles, update a world model with itself at the origin, and recalculate a trajectory given velocity projections. It can, instead, exploit the invariant relation between its current velocity and instantaneous time to contact obstacles in order to determine a new trajectory directly. It adapts its actions to changes in time to contact. If the environment is perceived in terms of actions that are *afforded* rather than in terms of objects and relations, the otherwise computationally intensive task is drastically simplified.

Now this is nothing short of a Ptolemaic revolution. If the world is always sensed from a perspective that views the environment as a space of possibilities for actions, then every time an agent performs an action that changes the action potentials the world affords it, it changes the world as it perceives it. In the last example, this occurs because as the agent changes its instantaneous speed and direction, it may perceive significant changes in environmental affordances despite being in almost the same spatial relations to objects in the environment. Even slight actions can change the way a creature perceives the world. If these changes in perception regularly simplify the problem of attaining goals, then traditional accounts of the environment as a static structure composed of objects, relations, and functions may completely misstate the actual computational problems faced by creatures acting in the world. The real problem must be defined relative to the world-for-the-agent. The world-for-the-agent changes despite the world-in-itself remaining constant.

To take another example of how action and perception are intertwined, and, so, must be considered when stating the computational problems facing agents, consider the problems of grasp planning. Traditionally the problem is defined as follows: Given a target object and an initial configuration of hand joints and free space between hand and target, find a trajectory of joint changes that results in a stable grasp. At one time it was thought that to solve this problem, it was necessary to compute the three dimensional shape of the target, the final configuration of joints, and the trajectory of joint changes between initial and final configurations — a substantial amount of computation by anyone's measure. Yet, this is not the problem if we allow compliance. Instead, we simply need to locate a rough center of mass of the target, send the palm of the hand to that point with the instruction to close on contact, and rely on the hand to comply with the object. The problem is elegantly simplified. No longer must we know the shape of the object, the mapping relation between three dimensional shape and joint configuration, or the constraints on joint closure. The original definition of the grasp planning problem was a misstatement. It led us to believe that certain subproblems and certain elements of knowledge would be required, when, in fact, they are not. Compliance changes everything. It alters the way the world should be interpreted.

The point is that the possibility of complying with shapes restructures the world. A creature with a compliant hand confronts a different world than a creature without. Accordingly, a knowledge level account of grasping that did not accommodate the simplifications due to compliance would be false. It would be working with an incorrect set of assumptions about the manipulator.

By analogy, one cardinal idea of the embodied approach to cognition is that the hardware of the body — in particular, the details of the sensorimotor system — when taken in conjunction with an environment and goals shapes the kinds of problems facing an agent. These problems, in turn, shape the cognitive skills agents have. Consequently, to specify these skills correctly, it is necessary to pay close attention to the agent's interactions with its environment — to the actions it does and can do at any point. Disembodied approaches do not interpret the environment of action in this dynamic manner and, so, inevitably give rise to false problems and false solutions. They tend to define problems in terms of task environments specified in the abstract perspective independent language of objects and relations.

Now this argument, it seems to me, is sound. However, how far does it go? It serves as a reminder to knowledge level theorists that they may easily misspecify a cognitive skill and that to reliably theorize at the knowledge level, one should often have a model of the agent's sensori-motor capabilities. However, it is an empirical question as to just how often hardware biases the definition of a cognitive problem. A priori, one would expect a continuum of problems from the most situated — where the cognitive task cannot be correctly defined without a careful analysis of the possible compliances and possible agent environment invariants — to highly abstract problems, such as word problems, number problems, puzzles, and so forth, where the task is essentially abstract and its implementation in the world is largely irrelevant to performance.

Ultimately, Brooks' rejections of disembodied artificial intelligence is an empirical challenge: for a large class of problems facing an acting creature, the only reliable method of discovering how they can succeed, and, hence, what their true cognitive skills are, is to study them in situ.

Frequently, this is the way of foundational questions. One theorist argues that many of the assumptions underpinning the prevailing methodology are false. He then proposes a new methodology and looks for empirical support.

However, occasionally, it is possible to offer, in addition to empirical support, a set of purely philosophical arguments against a methodology.

At the top level we may distinguish two philosophical objections: first, that knowledge level accounts that leave out a theory of the body are too incomplete to serve the purpose for which they were proposed. Second, that axiomatic knowledge accounts fail to capture all the knowledge an agent has about a domain. Let us consider each in turn.

The adequacy of a theory, whether in physics or artificial intelligence, depends on the purpose it is meant to serve. It is possible to identify three rather different purposes artificial intelligence theorists have in mind when they postulate a formal theory of the commonsense world. An axiomatic theory T of domain D is (1) adequate for *robotics* if it can be used by an acting perceiving machine to achieve its goals when operating in D; (2) adequate for a *disembodied rational planner* if it entails all and only the intuitive truths of D as expressed in the language of the user or the planner; and (3) adequate for *cognitive science* if it effectively captures the knowledge of D that actual agents have.

The philosophical arguments I will now present are meant to show that a formal theory of D, unless accompanied by a theory about the sensorimotor capacities of the creature using the theory, will fail no matter which purpose a theorist has in mind. Theories of conceptualization alone are inadequate; they require theories of embodiment.

According to Nilsson (1991), the touchstone of adequacy of a logicist theory is that it marks the necessary domain distinctions and makes the necessary domain predictions for an acting perceiving machine to achieve its goals. Theoretical adequacy is a function of four variables: D, the actual subject-independent properties of a domain; P, the creature's perceptual capacities; A, the creature's action repertoire; and G, the creature's goals. In principle, a change in any one of these can affect the theoretical adequacy of an axiomatization. For changes in perceptual abilities, no less than changes in action abilities or goals, may render domain distinctions worthless, invisible to a creature.

If axioms are adequate only relative to D P A G, then formal theories are, strictly speaking, untestable without an account of D P A G. We can never know whether a given axiom set captures the distinctions and relations that a particular robot will need for coping with D. We cannot just assume that T is adequate if it satisfies our own intuitions of the useful distinctions inherent in a domain. The intuitions we ourselves have about the domain will be relative to our own action repertoire, perceptual capacities, and goals. Nor will appeal to model theory help. Model theoretic interpretations only establish consistency. They say nothing about the appropriateness, truth, or utility of axiom sets for a given creature.

Moreover, this need to explicitly state A, P, and G is not restricted to robots or creatures having substantially different perceptual-motor capacities than our own. There is always the danger that between any two humans there are substantive differences about the intuitively useful distinctions inherent in the domain. The chemist, for instance, who wishes to axiomatize the knowledge a robot needs to cope with the many liquids it may encounter has, by dint of study, refined his observa-tional capacities to the point where he or she can notice theoretical properties of the liquid that remain invisible to the rest of us. They will use in their axiomatizations primitive terms that they believe are obser-vational. For most of us, they are not. We require axiomatic connections to tie those terms to more directly observational ones. As a result, there is, in all probability, a continuum of formal theories of the commonsense world ranging from ones understandable by novices to those understandable only by experts. Without an account of the observational capacities presupposed by a theory, however, it is an open question just which level of expertise a given T represents.

It may be objected that an account of the observational capacities supposed by a theory is not actually part of the theory but of the metatheory of use — the theory that explains how to *apply* the theory. However, this difference is in name alone. The domain knowledge that is required to tie a predicate to the observational conditions that are relevant to it is itself substantial. If a novice is to use the expert's theory, he or she will have to know how to make all things considered judgments about whether a given phenomenon is an A-type event or a B-type event. Similarly, if the expert is to use the novice's theory, he or she must, likewise, consult the novice's theory to decide the best way to collapse observational distinctions he or she notices. In either case, it is arbitrary where we say these world-linking axioms are to be found. They are part and parcel of domain knowledge, but they form the basis for a theory of embodiment (Kirsh, 1991, pp. 18–19).

The Third Assumption: The Accuracy of English or Symbolic Languages to Describe Cognitive Processes

In the following section, Kirsh (1991) questions whether computational languages are adequate to capture all varieties of cognition. In addition, Kirsh warns against the theorist's attribution to the machine of an understanding of the machine's language in the same way that the theorist understands the language.

I have been arguing that there are grave problems with the methodological assumption that cognitive skills can be studied in abstraction from the sensing and motor apparatus of the bodies that incorporate them. Both empirical and philosophical arguments can be presented to show that the body shows through. This does not vitiate the program of knowledge level theorists, but it does raise doubts about the probability of correctly modelling all cognitive skills on the knowledge-base/inference-engine model.

A further assumption related to disembodied AI is that we can use logic or English to track the trajectory of informational states a system creates as it processes a cognitive task. That is, either the predicate calculus or English can serve as a useful semantics for tracking the type of computation that goes on in cognition. They are helpful metalanguages.

From the logicist's point of view, when an agent computes its next behavior it creates a trajectory of informational states that are *about* the objects, functions and relations designated in the designer's conceptualization of the environment. This language is, of course, a logical language. Hence the transitions between these informational states can be described as *rational transitions* or inferences in that logical language. If English is the semantic metalanguage, then rational transitions between sentences will be less well-defined, but ought nonetheless to make sense as reasonable.

There are two defects with this approach. First, that it is parochial: that in fact there are many types of computation which are not amenable to characterization in a logical metalanguage, but which still count as cognition. Second, because it is easy for a designer to mistake his own conceptualization for a machine's conceptualization there is a tendency to misinterpret the machine's information trajectory, often attributing to the machine a deeper grasp of the world than is proper [italics added].

Argument 1. Consider the second objection first. As mentioned earlier, it is necessary to distinguish those cases where:

(1) the designer uses concepts to describe the environment which the machine does not understand and perhaps could not;
(2) the designer uses only those concepts which the machine grasps, but the two represent those concepts differently;
(3) both designer and machine use the same concepts and encode them in the same way.

The first two cases concern the appropriate metalanguage of design, the last the object language of processing. *Our goal as scientists is to represent a creature's cognition as accurately as possible, both so we can certify what it is doing, hence debug it better, and so we can design it better from the outset.*

The trouble that regularly arises, though, is that the designer has a conceptualization of the task environment that is quite distinct from that of the system [italics added]. There is always more than one way of *specifying* an ability, and more than one way of specifying an environment of action. Choice of a metalanguage should be made on pragmatic grounds: which formalism most simplifies the designer's task? *But lurking in the background is the worry that if the designer uses a metalanguage that invokes concepts the system simply does not or could not have, then he may propose mistaken designs which he later verifies as correct using the same incorrect metalanguage* [italics added].

For example, suppose we wish to design a procedure controlling a manipulator able to draw a circle on a crumpled piece of paper. The naive procedure will not produce a curve whose distance on the crumpled surface is equidistant. Its design works for flat surfaces, not for arbitrary surfaces. Yet if a system did have concepts for equidistance, locus and points, it ought to be *adaptive* enough to accommodate deformations in the surface topology. To be sure, such a machine would have to have some way of sensing topology. That by itself is not enough, though. It is its dispositions to behave in possible worlds that matters. This is shown by the old comment that whether I have the concept *chordate* (creature having a heart) or *renate* (creature having kidneys) cannot be determined by studying my normal behavior alone (Quine, 1960). In normal worlds, chordates are renates. Only in counter-factual worlds — where it is possible to come across viable creatures with hearts but no kidneys — could we display our individuating dispositions. *The upshot is that a designer cannot assume that his characterization of the informational trajectory of a creature is correct, unless he confirms certain claims about the creature's dispositions to behave in a range of further contexts. Sometimes these contexts lie outside the narrow task he is building a cognitive skill for* [italics added].

None of the above establishes that English is inadequate. It just shows that it is easy to make false attributions of content. The criticism that logic and natural language are not adequate metalanguages arises as soon as we ask whether they are expressive enough to describe some of the bizarre concepts systems which funny dispositions will have. *In principle, both logic and English are expressive*

*enough to capture any comprehensible concept. But the resulting character-
ization may be so long and confusing that it will be virtually incomprehensible*
[italics added]. For instance, if we try to identify what I have been calling the
implicit concepts of the compass controller we will be stymied. If the system
could talk, what would it say to the question: Can a *circle* be drawn in a space
measured with a non-Euclidian metric? What nascent idea of equidistance does
it have? *Its inferences would be so idiosyncratic that finding an English
sentence or reasonable axiomatic account would be out of the question. English
and logic are the wrong metalanguages to characterize such informational
states* [italics added].

What is needed is more in the spirit of a functional account of informational
content (Birnbaum, 1991). Such semantics are usually ugly. For in stating the
role an informational state plays in a system's dispositions to behave, we
characteristically need to mention myriad other states, since the contribution of
a state is a function of other states as well.

Accordingly, not all informational states are best viewed as akin to English
sentences. If we want to understand the full range of cognitive skills —
especially those modular ones which are not directly hooked up to central
inference — we will need to invoke some other language for describing
information content. Frequently the best way to track a computation is not as a
rational trajectory in a logical language.

Argument 2. *The need for new languages to describe informational content
has recently been reiterated by certain connectionists who see in parallel
distributing processing a different style of computation* [italics added]. Hewitt
and Gasser have also emphasized a similar need for an alternative understanding of the computational processes occurring in distributed AI systems. It
is old-fashioned and parochial to hope for a logic-based denotational semantics
for such systems.

The PDP [parallel distribution processing] concern can be stated as follows:
in PDP computation vectors of activation propagate through a partially
connected network. According to Smolensky (Schank & Riesbeck, 1981), it is
constructive to describe the behavior of the system as a path in tensor space.
The problem of interpretation is to characterize the significant events on this
path. It would be pleasing if we could say "now the network is extracting the
information that p, now the information that q," and so on, until the system
delivers its answer. *Unfortunately, though, except for input and output vectors
— whose interpretation we specifically set — the majority of vectors are not
interpretable as carrying information which can be easily stated in English or
logic. There need be no one-to-one mapping between significant events in the
system's tensor space trajectory and its path in propositional space. Smolensky
— whose argument this is — suggests that much of this intermediate processing
is interpretable at the subconceptual level where the basic elements of meaning
differ from those we have words for in English* [italics added].

One way of seeing the problem is to recognize that in a simple feed-forward network a given hidden unit can be correlated with a (possibly nested) disjunction of conjunctions of probabilities of input features. A vector, therefore, can be interpreted as a combination of these. The result is a compound that may make very little sense to us. For instance, it might correspond to a distribution over the entire feature set. Thus a single node might be tuned to respond to the weighted conjunction of features comprising the tip of my nose, my heel, plus the luminescence of my hands, or the weighted conjunction of. . . . Moreover, if we do not believe that the semantics of networks is correlational but rather functional we will prefer to interpret the meaning of a node to be its contribution (in conjunction with its superior nodes) to the capacity to classify.

In like manner, Hewitt and Gasser offer another argument for questioning whether we can track the information flowing through a complex system in propositional form. The question they ask is: How are we to understand the content of a message sent between two agents who are part of a much larger matrix of communicating agents? Superficially, each agent has its own limited perspective on the task. From agent-1's point of view, agent-2 is saying p; from agent-3's point of view, agent-2 is saying q. Is there a right answer? Is there a God's eye perspective that identifies the true content and gives the relativized perspective to each agent? If so, how is this relativized meaning to be determined? We will have to know not only whom the message is addressed to, but what the addressee is expecting, and what it can *do* with the message. Again, though, once we focus on the effects which messages have on a system, we leave the simple world of denotational semantics and opt for functional semantics. Just how we characterize *possible effects*, however, is very different than giving a translation of the message in English. We will need a language for describing the behavioral dispositions of agents.

Cognition as rational inference looks less universal once we leave the domain of familiar sequential processing and consider massively parallel architectures [italics added] [Kirsh, 1991, pp. 22–25].

The Fourth Assumption: The Separateness of Cognition from Learning

In the following section, Kirsh (1991) compares the claim of logicism that cognition is isolable from learning with the position of SOAR, PDP, and self-modifying systems.

In a pure top-down approach, we assume it is possible to state what a system knows without stating how it came to that knowledge. The two questions, competence and acquisition, can be separated. Learning, on this view, is a switch that can be turned on or off. It is a box that takes an early conceptualization and returns a more mature conceptualization. Thus, learning and conceptualization are sufficiently distinct that the two can be studied separately. Indeed, learning is often understood as the mechanism for generating a trajectory of conceptualizations. This is clearly the belief of logic theorists and developmental psychologists who maintain that what an agent knows at a given stage of development is a theory, not fundamentally different in spirit than a scientific theory, about the domain (Carey, 1985).

There are several problems with this view. First, it assumes we can characterize the instantaneous conceptualization of a system without having to study its various earlier conceptualizations. But what if we cannot *elicit* the system's conceptualization using the standard techniques? To determine what a competent PDP system, for example, would know about its environment of action, it is necessary to train it until it satisfies some adequacy metric. We cannot say in advance what the system will know if it is perfectly competent because there are very many paths to competence, each of which potentially culminates in a different solution. Moreover, if the account of PDP offered above is correct it may be impossible to characterize the system's conceptualization in a logical language or in English. It is necessary to analyze its dispositions. But to do that one needs an actual implementation displaying the competence. Hence the only way to know what a PDP system will know if it is competent, is to build one and study it. A purely top-down stance, which assumes that learning is irrelevant, is bound to fail in the case of PDP.

The second argument against detaching knowledge and learning also focuses on the *in practice* unpredictable nature of the learning trajectory. In SOAR it is frequently said that chunking is more than mere speedup (Rosenbloom, Laird, Newell, & McCarl, 1991). The results of repeatedly chunking solutions to impasses has a nonlinear effect on performance. Once we have nonlinear effects, however, we cannot predict the evolution of a system short of running it. Thus, in order to determine the steady state of knowledge underpinning a skill, we need to run SOAR with its chunking module on.

A final reason we cannot study what a system knows without studying how it acquired that knowledge is that a system may have special design features that let it acquire knowledge. It is organized to self-modify. Hence we cannot predict what knowledge it may contain unless we know how it integrates new information with old. There are many ways to self-modify.

For instance, according to Roger Schank, much of the knowledge a system contains is lodged in its indexing scheme (Schank & Riesbeck, 1981). As systems grow in size, they generally have to revise their indexing scheme. The results of this process of revision cannot be anticipated a priori unless we have a good idea of the earlier indexing schemes. The reason is that much of its knowledge is stored in cases. Case knowledge may be sensitive to the order in which the cases were encountered. Consequently, we can never determine the knowledge a competent system has unless we know something of the cases it was exposed to and the order in which they were met. History counts.

This emphasis on cases goes along with a view that much of reasoning involves noticing analogies to past experiences. A common corollary to this position is that concepts are not context-free intentions; they have a certain open texture, making it possible to flexibly extend their use and to apply them to new situations in creative ways. An agent which understands a concept should be able to recognize and generate analogical extensions of its concepts to new contexts.

Once we view concepts to be open-textured, however, it becomes plausible to suppose that a concept's meaning is a function of history. It is easier to see an analogical extension of a word if it has already been extended in that direction before. But then, we can't say what an agent's concept of "container" is unless we know the variety of contexts it has seen the word in. If that is so, it is impossible to understand a creature's conceptualization in abstraction from its learning history. *Much of cognition cannot be studied independently of learning* [italics added] [Kirsh, 1991, pp. 25–27].

The Fifth Assumption: The Uniformity of Cognitive Architecture

The strong claim of Newell (1991) that the SOAR system unifies all of cognition by means of a small set of mechanisms within a uniform architecture is critically analyzed by Kirsh (1991) in the following account.

The final issue I will discuss is the claim made by Newell et al. that cognition is basically the product of running programs in a single architecture. According to Newell, too much of the research in AI and cognitive science aims at creating independent representational and control mechanisms for solving particular cognitive tasks. Each investigator has his or her preferred computational models which, clever as they may be, rarely meet a further constraint that they be integratable into a unified account of cognition. For Newell:

Psychology has arrived at the possibility of unified theories of cognition — theories that gain their power by positioning a single system of mechanisms that operate together to produce the full range of human cognition. (Newell, 1991)

The idea that there might be a general theory of intelligence is not new. At an abstract level anyone who believes that domain knowledge plus inferential abilities are responsible for intelligent performance, at least in one sense, operates with a general theory of cognition. For, on that view, it is knowledge, ultimately, that is the critical element in cognition.

But Newell's claim is more concrete: not only is knowledge the basis for intelligence; knowledge, he argues further, will be encoded in a SOAR-like mechanism. This claim goes well beyond what most logicists would maintain. It is perfectly consistent with logicism that knowledge may be encoded, implemented or embedded in any of dozens of ways. A bare commitment to specification of cognitive skills at the knowledge level is hardly grounds for expecting a small set of "underlying mechanisms, whose interactions and compositions provide the answers to all the questions we have — predictions, explanations, designs, controls" (Newell, 1991) pertaining to the full range of cognitive performances. The SOAR project, however, is predicated on this very possibility. The goal of the group is to test the very strong claim that under-pinning problem solving, decision making, routine action, memory, learning, skill, even perception and motor behavior, there is a single architecture, "a single system [that] produces all aspects of behavior. . . . Even if the mind has parts, modules, components, or whatever, they mesh together" and work in accordance with a small set of principles.

It is not my intent to provide serious arguments for or against this position. I mention it largely because it is such a deep commitment of the SOAR research program and therefore an assumption that separates research orientations. The strongest support for it must surely be empirical, and it will become convincing only as the body of evidence builds up. There can be little doubt, though, that it is an assumption not universally shared.

Minsky, for instance, in his book *Society of Mind* (1986), has argued that intelligence is the product of hundreds, probably thousands of specialized computational mechanisms he terms agents. There is no homogeneous under-lying architecture. In the society of mind theory, mental activity is the product of many agents of varying complexity interacting in hundreds of ways. The very purpose of the theory is to display the variety of mechanisms that are likely to be useful in a mind-like system, and to advocate the need for diversity. Evolution, Minsky emphasizes is an opportunistic tinkerer likely to co-opt existing mechanisms in an *ad hoc* manner to create new functions meeting new needs. With such diversity and ad hoccery it would be surprising if most cognitive performances were the result of a few mechanisms comprising a principled architecture.

Brooks in a similar manner sets out to recreate intelligent capacities by building layer upon layer of mechanism, each with hooks into lower layers to suppress or bias input and output. Again, no non-empirical arguments may be offered to convince skeptics of the correctness of this view. The best that has been offered is that the brain seems to have diverse mechanisms of behaviour control, so it is plausible that systems with comparable functionality will too.

Again there is no quick way to justify the assumption of architecture homogeneity. More than any other foundational issue this is one for which non-empirical or philosophical arguments are misplaced [italics added] [Kirsh, 1991, pp. 27–28].

The Foundational Assumptions: Conclusions

Kirsh (1991) concludes his discussion of the preeminent foundational issues of artificial intelligence in the following terms.

I have presented five dimensions — five big issues — which theorists in AI, either tacitly or explicitly, take a stand on. Any selection of issues is bound to have a personal element to them. In my case I have focussed most deeply on the challenges of embodiment. How reliable can theories of cognition be if they assume that systems can be studied abstractly, without serious concern for the mechanisms that ground a system's conceptualization in perception and action? But other more traditional issues are of equal interest. How central is the role which knowledge plays in cognitive skills? Can most of cognition be seen as inference? What part does learning or psychological development play in the studying of reasoning and performance? Will a few mechanisms of control and representation suffice for general intelligence? *None of the arguments presented here even begin to be decisive. Nor were they meant to be. Their function is to encourage informed debate of the paramount issues informing our field* [italics added] [Kirsh, 1991, pp. 28–29].

Commentary

It is useful to analyze the abstract assumptions of intelligence and intelligent systems in two categories: strategic cognition and automatic cognition.

Strategic Cognition

At the human level, strategic cognition has its clearest manifestation in lucid deliberative conscious thought directed toward a difficult intellectual problem. Knowledge, inference, and verbal, mathematical, or spatial language are required. At the system level, strategic cognition is similar except for the quality of consciousness. Applicatory here are Kirsh's first and third fundamental assumptions:

— *Pre-eminence of knowledge and conceptualization*: Intelligence that transcends insect-level intelligence requires declarative knowledge and some form of reasoning-like computation — call this *cognition*. Core AI is the study of the conceptualizations of the world presupposed and used by intelligent systems during cognition.
— *Kinematics of cognition are language-like*: It is possible to describe the trajectory of knowledge states or informational states created during cognition using a vocabulary very much like English or some regimented logico-mathematical version of English [Kirsh, 1991, p. 4].

Automatic Cognition

At the human level, "automatic cognition" refers to unconscious and proceduralized mechanisms of language, thought, and memory. At the system level, automatic cognition is similar except for the quality of unconsciousness. Applicatory here are the neurally inspired concepts of connectionism and the mathematically inspired finite state models of roboticism.

A complete theory of intelligence and intelligent systems will need to account for both strategic cognition and automatic cognition. The attainment of such a theory represents one of the most formidable problems in all of science.

THEORIES OF UNIFIED COGNITION

Newell's Unified Theory and the SOAR Research Project

In the following passage from his theoretical and research volume *Unified Theories of Cognition*, Newell (1990) presents his position on the unitary nature of cognition as derivative from a small set of basic mechanisms.

Psychology has arrived at the possibility of unified theories of cognition — theories that gain their power by having a single system of mechanisms that operate together to produce the full range of cognition.

I do not say they are here. But they are within reach and we should strive to attain them [Newell, 1990, p. 1].

The "single system of mechanisms" is a central objective of the SOAR research program (Rosenbloom et al., 1991).

Theoretical Background of SOAR

Rosenbloom and colleagues (1991) discuss the general theoretical background of the SOAR system and its relationship to human and artificial intelligence.

The central scientific problem of artificial intelligence (AI) is to understand what constitutes intelligent action and what processing organizations are capable of such action. Human intelligence — which stands before us like a holy grail — shows to first observation what can only be termed general intelligence. A single human exhibits a bewildering diversity of intelligent behavior. The types of goals that humans can set for themselves or accept from the environment seem boundless. Further observation, of course, shows limits to this capacity in any individual — problems range from easy to hard, and problems can always be found that are too hard to be solved. But the general point is still compelling.

Work in AI has already contributed substantially to our knowledge of what functions are required to produce general intelligence. There is substantial, though certainly not unanimous, agreement about some functions that need to be supported: symbols and goal structures, for example. Less agreement exists about what mechanisms are appropriate to support these functions, in large part because such matters depend strongly on the rest of the system and on cost-benefit tradeoffs. Much of this work has been done under the rubric of AI tools and languages, rather than AI systems themselves. However, it takes only a slight shift of viewpoint to change from what is an aid for the programmer to what is structure for the intelligent system itself. Not all creatures survive this transformation, but enough do to make the development of AI languages as much substantial research as tool building. These proposals provide substantial ground on which to build.

The SOAR project has been building on this foundation in an attempt to understand the functionality required to support general intelligence. Our current understanding is embodied in the SOAR architecture (Laird, 1986; Laird, Rosenbloom, and Newell, 1986) [italics added] [Rosenbloom et al., 1991, pp. 289–290].

General Intelligence and Levels of Description

Rosenbloom and colleagues (1991) analyze general intelligence at several levels of description, employing the concepts of cognitive, neural, and logical bands.

The idea of analyzing systems in terms of multiple levels of description is a familiar one in computer science. In one version, computer systems are described as a sequence of levels that starts at the bottom with the device level and works up through the circuit level, the logic level, and then one or more program levels. Each level provides a description of the system at some level of abstraction. The sequence is built up by defining each higher level in terms of the structure provided at the lower levels. This idea has also recently been used to analyze human cognition in terms of levels of description (Newell, 1990). Each level corresponds to a particular time scale, such as ~100 msec. and ~1 sec., with a new level occurring for each new order of magnitude. *The four levels between ~10 msec. and ~10 sec. comprise the cognitive band [Fig. 1.1].* The lowest cognitive level — at ~10 msec. — is the symbol-accessing level, where the knowledge referred to by symbols is retrievable. The second cognitive level — at ~100 msec. — is the level at which elementary deliberate operations occur; that is, the level at which encoded knowledge is brought to bear, and the most elementary choices are made. The third and fourth cognitive levels — at ~1 sec. and ~10 sec. — are the simple-operator-composition and goal-attainment levels. At these levels, sequences of deliberations can be composed to achieve goals. *Above the cognitive band is the rational band, at which the system can be described as being goal oriented, knowledge-based, and strongly adaptive. Below the cognitive band is the neural band.*

FIGURE 1.1
Partial Hierarchy of Time Scales in Human Cognition

The SOAR architecture as a basis for general intelligence

Rational Band	...	
Cognitive Band	~10 sec.	Goal attainment
	~1 sec.	Simple operator composition
	~100 msec.	Elementary deliberate operations
	~10 msec.	Symbol accessing
Neural Band	...	

Source: Rosenbloom, P. S., Laird, J. E., Newell, A., and McCarl, R. (1991). A preliminary analysis of the SOAR architecture as a basis for general intelligence. *Artificial Intelligence*, *47*, 289–325. Reprinted with the permission of the Elsevier Science Publishers.

[We] describe SOAR as a sequence of three cognitive levels: the memory level, at which symbol accessing occurs; the decision level, at which elementary deliberate operations occur; and the goal level, at which goals are set and achieved via sequences of decisions. The goal level is an amalgamation of the top two cognitive levels from the analysis of human cognition.

In this description we will often have call to describe mechanisms that are built into the architecture of SOAR. *The architecture consists of all of the fixed structure of the SOAR system. According to the levels of analysis, the correct view to be taken of this fixed structure is that it comprises the set of mechanisms provided by the levels underneath the cognitive band. For human cognition this is the neural band. For artificial cognition, this may be a connectionist band, though it need not be. This view notwithstanding, it should be remembered that it is the SOAR architecture which is primary in our research. The use of the levels viewpoint is simply an attempt at imposing a particular, hopefully illuminating, theoretical structure on top of the existing architecture* [italics added] [Rosenbloom et al., 1991, pp. 290–291].

SOAR: The First Methodological Assumption

The development of SOAR rests on four methodological assumptions (Table 1.2). The first of these four assumptions is described in the following section.

TABLE 1.2
SOAR's Methodological Assumptions

1. General intelligence comprises neural, cognitive, and rational levels or bands. SOAR concentrates on the cognitive band.
2. A theory of general intelligence embraces both human and artificial intelligence.
3. The intelligence of SOAR results from a small set of mechanisms.
4. Research should utilize SOAR's existing mechanisms in exploring new areas of application rather than adding new mechanisms.

The first assumption is the utility of focusing on the cognitive band, as opposed to the neural or rational bands. This is a view that has traditionally been shared by a large segment of the cognitive science community; it is not, however, shared by the connectionist community, which focuses on the neural band (plus the lower levels of the cognitive band), or by the logicist and expert-systems communities, which focus on the rational band. This assumption is not meant to be exclusionary, as a complete understanding of general intelligence requires the understanding of all these descriptive bands (Investigations of the relationship of SOAR to the neural and rational bands can be found in Newell, 1990; Rosenbloom, 1989; and Rosenbloom, Newell, and Laird, 1990). Instead the assumption is that there is important work to be done by focusing on the cognitive band. One reason is that, as just mentioned, a complete model of general intelligence will require a model of the cognitive band. A second reason is that an understanding of the cognitive band can constrain models of the neural and rational bands. A third, more applied reason, is that a model of the cognitive band is required in order to be able to build practical intelligence systems. Neural-band models need the higher levels of organization that are provided by the cognitive band in order to reach complex task performance. Rational-band models need the heuristic adequacy provided by the cognitive band in order to be computationally feasible. *A fourth reason is that there is a wealth of both psychological and AI data about the cognitive band that can be used as the basis for elucidating the structure of its levels. This data can help us understand what type of symbolic architecture is required to support general intelligence* [italics added] [Rosenbloom et al., 1991, pp. 291–292].

SOAR: The Second Methodological Assumption

The second methodological assumption concerns the benefits that accrue from a conception of general intelligence that includes both human and artificial intelligence.

The second assumption is that general intelligence can most usefully be studied by not making a distinction between human and artificial intelligence. The advantage of this assumption is that it allows wider ranges of research methodologies and data to be brought to bear to mutually constrain the structure of the system. Our research methodology includes a mixture of experimental data, theoretical justifications, and comparative studies in both artificial intelligence and cognitive psychology. Human experiments provide data about performance universals and limitations that may reflect the structure of the architecture. For example, the ubiquitous power law of practice — the time to perform a task is a power-law function of the number of times the task has been performed — was used to generate a model of human practice (Newell and Rosenbloom, 1981; Rosenbloom and Newell, 1986), which later converted into a proposal for a general artificial learning mechanism (Laird, Rosenbloom, and Newell, 1984, 1986; Steier et al., 1987). Artificial experiments — the application of implemented systems to a variety of tasks requiring intelligence — provide sufficient feedback about the mechanisms embodied in the architecture and their interactions (Hsu, Prietula, and Steier, 1988; Rosenbloom et al., 1985; Steier, 1987; Steier and Newell, 1988; Washington and Rosenbloom, 1988). Theoretical justifications attempt to provide an abstract analysis of the requirements of intelligence, and of how various architectural mechanisms fulfill those requirements (Newell, 1990; Newell, Rosenbloom, and Laird, 1989; Rosenbloom, 1989; Rosenbloom, Laird, and Newell, 1988; Rosenbloom, Newell, and Laird, 1990). Comparative studies pitting one system against another, provide an evaluation of how well the respective systems perform, as well as insight about how the capabilities of one of the systems can be incorporated in the other (Etzioni and Mitchell, 1989; Rosenbloom and Laird, 1986) [italics added] [Rosenbloom et al., 1991, p. 292].

SOAR: The Third Methodological Assumption

The third methodological assumption posits a small set of mechanisms to be sufficient for the SOAR architecture to function intelligently.

The third assumption is that the architecture should consist of a small set of orthogonal mechanisms. All intelligent behaviors should involve all, or nearly all, of these basic mechanisms. This assumption biases the development of SOAR strongly in the direction of uniformity and simplicity, and away from modularity (Fodor, 1983) and toolkit approaches. When attempting to achieve a new functionality in SOAR, the first step is to determine in what ways the existing mechanisms can already provide the functionality. This can force the development of new solutions to old problems, and reveal new connections — through the common underlying mechanisms — among previously distinct capabilities (Rosenbloom, Laird, and Newell, 1988). Only if there is no appropriate way to achieve the new functionality are new mechanisms considered [italics added] [Rosenbloom et al., 1991, p. 293].

SOAR: The Fourth Methodological Assumption

The fourth methodological assumption is that the SOAR system should be maximally stretched to expand its range of intelligent performance.

The fourth assumption is that architectures should be pushed to the extreme to evaluate how much of general intelligence they can cover. A serious attempt at evaluating the coverage of an architecture involves a long-term commitment by an extensive research group. Much of the research involves the apparently mundane activity of replicating classical results within the architecture. Sometimes these demonstrations will by necessity be strict replications, but often the architecture will reveal novel approaches, provide a deeper under-standing of the result and test relationship to other results, or provide the means of going beyond what was done in the classical work. *As these results accumulate over time, along with other more novel results, the system gradually approaches the ultimate goal of general intelligence* [italics added] [Rosenbloom et al., 1991, p. 293].

Structure of SOAR: Memory Level

SOAR's declarative, procedural, control, and episodic knowledge are stored in a long-term memory production and can be retrieved for processing in working memory.

Long-Term Memory

Major characteristics of SOAR's long-term memory are described in the following account.

A general intelligence requires a memory with a large capacity for the storage of knowledge. A variety of types of knowledge must be stored, including declarative knowledge (facts about the world, including facts about actions that can be performed), procedural knowledge (facts about how to perform actions, and control knowledge about which actions to perform when), and episodic knowledge (which actions were done when). Any particular task will require some subset of the knowledge stored in the memory. Memory access is the process by which this subset is retrieved for use in task performance.

The lowest level of the SOAR architecture is the level at which these memory phenomena occur. *All of SOAR's long term knowledge is stored in a single production memory. Whether a piece of knowledge represents proce-dural, declarative, or episodic knowledge, it is stored in one or more productions.* Each production is a condition-action structure that performs its actions when its conditions are met. Memory access consists of the execution of these productions. During the execution of a production, variables in its actions are instantiated with values. Action variables that existed in the conditions are instantiated with the values bound in the conditions. Action variables that did not exist in the conditions act as generators of new symbols [italics added] [Rosenbloom et al., 1991, pp. 293–294].

Working Memory

Important features and functions of SOAR's working memory are summarized in the following section.

The result of memory access is the retrieval of information into a global working memory. The working memory is a temporary memory that contains all of SOAR's short-term processing context. Working memory consists of an interrelated set of objects with attribute-value pairs. For example, an object representing a green cat named Fred might look like (objecto025 name fred type cat color green). The symbol o025 is the identifier of the object, a short-term symbol for the object that exists only as long as the object is in working memory. Objects are related by using the identifiers of some objects as attributes and values of other objects.

There is one special type of working memory structure, the preference. Preferences encode control knowledge about the acceptability and desirability of actions, according to a fixed semantics of preference types. Acceptability preferences determine which actions should be considered as candidates. Desirability preferences define a partial ordering on the candidate actions. For example, a better (or alternatively, worse) preference can be used to represent the knowledge that one action is more (or less) desirable than another action, and a best (or worst) preference can be used to represent the knowledge that an action is at least as good (or bad) as every other action [italics added] [Rosenbloom et al., 1991, p. 294].

Memory and Productions

The retrieval operations of SOAR's productions are set forth in the following account.

In a traditional production-system architecture, each production is a problem-solving operator (see, for example, [Nilsson, 1980]). The right-hand side of the production represents some action to be performed, and the left-hand side represents the preconditions for correct application of the action (plus possibly some desirability conditions). One consequence of this view of productions is that the productions must also be the locus of behavioral control. If productions are going to act, it must be possible to control which one executes at each moment, a process known as conflict resolution. In a logic architecture, each production is a logical implication. The meaning of such a production is that if the left-hand side (the antecedent) is true, then so is the right-hand side (the consequent). (The directionality of the implication is reversed in logic programming languages such as PROLOG, but the point still holds.) SOAR's productions are neither operators nor implications. Instead, SOAR's productions perform (parallel) memory retrieval. Each production is a retrieval structure for an item in long-term memory. The right-hand side of the rule represents a long-term datum, and the left-hand side represents the situations in which it is appropriate to retrieve that datum into working memory. The traditional production-system and logic notions of action, control, and truth are not directly applicable to SOAR's productions. All control in SOAR is performed at the decision level. *Thus, there is no conflict resolution process in the SOAR production system, and all productions execute in parallel. This all flows directly from the production system being a long-term memory. SOAR separates the retrieval of long-term information from the control of which act to perform next* [italics added] [Rosenbloom et al., 1991, pp. 294–295].

Encoding Knowledge in Productions

The rationale for SOAR's method of encoding declarative and procedural knowledge in productions is given in the following passage.

Of course it is possible to encode knowledge of operators and logical implications in the production memory. For example, the knowledge about how to implement a typical operator can be stored procedurally as a set of productions which retrieve the state resulting from the operator's application. The productions' conditions determine when the state is to be retrieved — for example, when the operator is being applied and its preconditions are met. An alternative way to store operator implementation knowledge is declaratively as a set of structures that are completely contained in the actions of one or more productions. The structures describe not only the results of the operator, but also its preconditions. The productions' conditions determine when to retrieve this declarative operator description into working memory. A retrieved operator description must be interpreted by other productions to actually have an effect.

In general, there are these two distinct ways to encode knowledge in the production memory: procedurally and declaratively. If the knowledge is procedurally encoded, then the execution of the production reflects the knowledge, but does not actually retrieve it into working memory — it only retrieves the structures encoded in the actions. On the other hand, if a piece of knowledge is encoded declaratively in the actions of a production, then it is retrievable in its entirety. *This distinction between procedural and declarative encodings of knowledge is distinct from whether the knowledge is declarative (represents facts about the world) or procedural (represents facts about procedures). Moreover, each production can be viewed in either way, either as a procedure which implicitly represents conditional information, or as the indexed storage of declarative structures* [italics added] [Rosenbloom et al., 1991, p. 295].

Structure of SOAR: Decision Level

The capacity to execute an appropriate course of action depends on its decision structures and functions as described in the following account.

In addition to a memory, a general intelligence requires the ability to generate and/or select a course of action that is responsive to the current situation. The second level of the SOAR architecture, the decision level, is the level at which this processing is performed. The decision level is based on the memory level plus an architecturally provided, fixed, decision procedure. The decision level proceeds in a two phase elaborate-decide cycle. During elaboration, the memory is accessed repeatedly, in parallel, until quiescence is reached; that is, until no more productions can execute. This results in the retrieval into working memory of all of the accessible knowledge that is relevant to the current decision. This may include a variety of types of information, but most direct relevance here is knowledge about actions that can be performed and preference knowledge about what actions are acceptable and desirable. After quiescence has occurred, the decision procedure selects one of the retrieved actions based on the preferences that were retrieved into working memory and their fixed semantics.

The decision level is open both with respect to the consideration of arbitrary actions, and with respect to the utilization of arbitrary knowledge in making a selection. This openness allows SOAR to behave in both plan-following and reactive fashions. SOAR is following a plan when a decision is primarily based on previously generated knowledge about what to do. SOAR is being reactive when a decision is based primarily on knowledge about the current situation (as reflected in the working memory) [italics added] [Rosenbloom, et al., 1991, pp. 295–296].

Structure of SOAR: Goal Level

The nature of goal setting and goal processing is described in the following section.

In addition to being able to make decisions, a general intelligence must also be able to direct this behavior towards some end; that is, it must be able to set and work towards goals. The third level of the SOAR architecture, the goal level, is the level at which goals are processed. This level is based on the decision level. Goals are set whenever a decision cannot be made; that is, when the decision procedure reaches an impasse. Impasses occur when there are no alternatives that can be selected (*no-change* and *rejection* impasses) or when there are multiple alternatives that can be selected, but insufficient discriminating preferences exist to allow a choice to be made among them (*tie* and *conflict* impasses). Whenever an impasse occurs, the architecture generates the goal of resolving the impasse. Along with this goal, a new *performance context* is created. The creation of a new context allows decisions to continue to be made in the service of achieving the goal of resolving the impasse — nothing can be done in the original context because it is at an impasse. If an impasse now occurs in this subgoal, another new subgoal and performance context are created. This leads to a goal (and context) stack in which the top-level goal is to perform some task, and lower-level goals are to resolve impasses in problem solving. A subgoal is terminated when either its impasse is resolved, or some higher impasse in the stack is resolved (making the subgoal superfluous) [italics added] [Rosenbloom et al., 1991, p. 296].

Goal activities are processed in problem spaces, as described in the following account.

In SOAR, all symbolic goal-oriented tasks are formulated in problem spaces. A problem space consists of a set of states and a set of operators. The states represent situations, and the operators represent actions which when applied to states yield other states. Each performance context consists of a goal, plus roles for a problem state, a state, and an operator. Problem solving is driven by decisions that result in the selection of problem spaces, states, and operators for their respective context roles. Given a goal, a problem space should be selected in which goal achievement can be pursued. Then an initial state should be selected that represents the initial situation. Then an operator should be selected for application to the initial state. Then another state should be selected (most likely the result of applying the operator to the previous state). This process continues until a sequence of operators has been discovered that transforms the initial state into a state in which the goal has been achieved. One subtle consequence of the use of problem spaces is that each one implicitly defines a set of constraints on how the task is to be performed. For example, if the Eight Puzzle is attempted in a problem space containing only a slide-tile operator, all solution paths maintain the constraint that the tiles are never picked up off the board. Thus, such conditions need not be tested explicitly in desired states.

Each problem solving decision — the selection of a problem space, a state, or an operator — is based on the knowledge accessible in the production memory. If the knowledge is both correct and sufficient, SOAR exhibits highly controlled behavior; at each decision point the right alternative is selected. Such behavior is accurately described as being algorithmic or knowledge-intensive. However, for a general intelligence faced with a broad array of unpredictable tasks, situations will arise — inevitably and indeed frequently — in which the accessible knowledge is either incorrect or insufficient. It is possible that correct decisions will fortuitously be made, but it is more likely that either incorrect decisions will be made or an impasse will occur. If an incorrect decision is made, the system must eventually recover and get itself back on a path to a goal, for example, by backtracking. If instead an impasse occurs, the system must execute a sequence of problem space operators in the resulting subgoal to find (or generate) the information that will allow a decision to be made. This processing may itself be highly algorithmic, if enough control knowledge is available to uniquely determine what to do, or it may involve a large amount of further search.

As described earlier, operator implementation knowledge can be represented procedurally in the production memory, enabling operator implementation to be performed directly by memory retrieval. When the operator is selected, a set of productions execute that collectively build up the representation of the result state by combining data from long-term memory and the previous state. This type of implementation is comparable to the conventional implementation of an operator as a fixed piece of code. However, if operator implementation knowledge is stored declaratively, or if no operator implementation knowledge is stored, then a subgoal occurs, and the operator must be implemented by the execution of a sequence of problem space operators in the subgoal. If a declarative description of the to-be-implemented operator is available, then these lower operations may implement the operator by interpreting its declarative description (as was demonstrated in work on task acquisition in SOAR (Steier et al., 1987)). Otherwise the operator can be implemented by decomposing it into a set of simpler operators for which operator implementation knowledge is available, or which can in turn be decomposed further.

When an operator is implemented in a subgoal, the combination of the operator and the subgoal correspond to the type of deliberately created subgoal common in AI problem solvers. The operator specifies a task to be performed, while the subgoal indicates that accomplishing the task should be treated as a goal for further problem solving. In complex problems, like computer configuration, it is common for there to be complex high-level operators, such as

Configure-computer, which are implemented by selecting problem spaces in which they can be decomposed into simpler tasks. Many of the traditional goal management issues — such as conjunction, conflict, and selection — show up as operator management issues in SOAR. For example, a set of conjunctive subgoals can be ordered by ordering operators that later lead to impasses (and subgoals).

As described in [Rosenbloom, Laird, and Newell, 1988], a subgoal not only represents a subtask to be performed, but it also represents an introspective act that allows unlimited amounts of meta-level problem-space processing to be performed. The entire working memory — the goal stack and all information linked to it — is available for examination and augmentation in a subgoal. At any time a production can examine and augment any part of the goal stack. Likewise, a decision can be made at any time for any of the goals in the hierarchy. This allows subgoal problem solving to analyze the situation that led to the impasse, and even to change the subgoal, should it be appropriate. One not uncommon occurrence is for information to be generated within a subgoal that instead of satisfying the subgoal, causes the subgoal to become irrelevant and consequently to disappear. Processing tends to focus on the bottom-most goal because all of the others have reached impasses. However, the processing is completely opportunistic, so that when appropriate information becomes available at a higher level, processing at that level continues immediately and all lower subgoals are terminated [italics added] [Rosenbloom et al., 1991, pp. 297–298].

Learning in SOAR

The concept of chunks and their nature, content, and role in learning are summarized in the following account.

All learning occurs by the acquisition of chunks — productions that summarize the problem solving that occurs in subgoals [Laird, Rosenbloom, and Newell, 1986]. The actions of a chunk represent the knowledge generated during the subgoal; that is, the results of the subgoal. The conditions of the chunk represent an access path to this knowledge, consisting of those elements of the parent goals upon which the results depended. The results of the subgoal are determined by finding the elements generated in the subgoal that are available for use in subgoals — an element is a result of a subgoal precisely because it is available to processes outside of the subgoal. The access path is computed by analyzing the traces of the productions that fired in the subgoal — each production trace effectively states that its actions depended on its conditions. This dependency analysis yields a set of conditions that have been implicitly generalized to ignore irrelevant aspects of the situation. The resulting generality allows chunks to transfer to situations other than the one in which it was learned. The primary system-wide effect of chunking is to move SOAR along the space-time trade-off by allowing relevantly similar future decisions to be based on direct retrieval of information from memory rather than on problem solving within a subgoal. If the chunk is used, an impasse will not occur, because the required information is already available.

Care must be taken to not confuse the power of chunking as a learning mechanism with the power of SOAR as a learning system. Chunking is a simple goal-based, dependency-tracing, caching scheme, analogous to explanation-based learning (DeJong and Mooney, 1986; Mitchell, Keller, and Kedar-Cabelli, 1986; Rosenbloom and Laird, 1986) and a variety of other schemes (Rosenbloom and Newell, 1986). *What allows SOAR to exhibit a wide variety of learning behaviors are the variations in the types of subgoals that are chunked; the types of problem solving, in conjunction with the types and sources of knowledge, used in the subgoals; and the ways the chunks are used in later problem solving. The role that a chunk will play is determined by the type of subgoal for which it was learned.* State-no-change, operator-tie, and operator-no-change subgoals lead respectively to state augmentation, operator selection, and operator implementation productions. *The content of a chunk is determined by the types of problem solving and knowledge used in the subgoal. A chunk can lead to skill acquisition if it is used as a more efficient means of generating an already generatable result. A chunk can lead to knowledge acquisition (or knowledge level learning (Dietterich, 1986)) if it is used to make old/new judgements; that is, to distinguish what has been learned from what has not been learned (Rosenbloom, Laird, and Newell, 1987, 1988)* [italics added] [Rosenbloom et al., 1991, pp. 298–299].

Perception and Motor Control in SOAR

The perceptual motor interface and its relationship to working memory are described in the following section.

One of the most recent functional additions to the SOAR architecture is a perceptual-motor interface (Weismeyer, 1988, 1989). All perceptual and motor behavior is mediated through working memory; specifically, through the state in the top problem solving context. Each distinct perceptual field has a designated attribute of this state to which it adds its information. Likewise, each distinct motor field has a designated attribute of the state from which it takes its commands. The perceptual and motor systems are autonomous with respect to each other and the cognitive system.

Encoding and decoding productions can be used to convert between the high-level structures used by the cognitive system, and the low-level structures used by the perceptual and motor systems. These productions are like ordinary productions, except that they examine only the perceptual and motor fields, and not any of the rest of the context stack. This autonomy from the context stack is critical, because it allows the decision procedure to proceed without waiting for quiescence among the encoding and decoding productions, which may never happen in a rapidly changing environment [Rosenbloom et al., 1991, pp. 299–300].

Default Knowledge in SOAR

The default knowledge in SOAR permits it to resolve impasses in its operations.

SOAR has a set of productions (55 in all) that provide default responses to each of the possible impasses that can arise, and thus prevent the system from dropping into a bottomless pit in which it generates an unbounded number of content-free performance contexts. . . . This allows another candidate operator to be selected, if there is one, or for a different impasse to arise if there are no additional candidates. This default response, as with all of them, can be overridden by additional knowledge if it is available.

One large part of the default knowledge (10 productions) is responsible for setting up large operator subgoaling as the default response to no-change impasses on operators. That is, it attempts to find some other state in the problem space to which the selected operators can be applied. This is accomplished by generating acceptable and worst preferences in the subgoal for the parent problem space. If another problem space is suggested, possibly for implementing the operator, it will be selected. Otherwise, the selection of the parent problem space in the subgoal enables operator subgoaling. A sequence of operators is then applied in the subgoal until a state is generated that satisfies the preconditions of an operator higher in the goal stack.

Another large part of the default knowledge (33 productions) is responsible for setting up look ahead search as the default response to tie impasses. This is accomplished by generating acceptable and worst preferences for the *selection* problem space. The selection problem space consists of operators that evaluate the tied alternatives. Based on the evaluations produced by these operators, default productions create preferences that break the tie and resolve the impasse. In order to apply the evaluation operators, domain knowledge must exist that can create an evaluation. If no such knowledge is available, a second impasse arises — a no-change on the evaluation operator. As mentioned earlier, the default response to an operator no-change impasse is to perform operator subgoaling. However, for a no-change impasse on an evaluation operator this is overridden and a look ahead search is performed instead. The results of the look ahead search are used to evaluate the tied alternatives.

As SOAR is developed, it is expected that more and more knowledge will be included as part of the basic system about how to deal with a variety of situations. For example, one area on which we are currently working is the provision of SOAR with a basic arithmetical capability, including problem spaces for addition, multiplication, subtraction, division, and comparison. One way of looking at existing default knowledge is as the tip of this large iceberg of background knowledge. However, another way to look at the default knowledge is as part of the architecture itself. Some of the default knowledge — how much is still unclear —must be innate rather than learned. The rest of the system's knowledge, such as the arithmetic spaces, should then be learnable from there [italics added] [Rosenbloom et al., 1991, pp. 300–301].

SOAR: Task Achievements

SOAR's achievements in search-based tasks are summarized in the following section (Table 1.3).

Various versions of SOAR have been demonstrated to be able to perform over 30 different search methods (Laird, 1986; Laird and Newell, 1983; Laird, Newell, and Rosenbloom, 1987). SOAR can also exhibit hybrid methods — such as a combination of hill-climbing and depth-first search or of operator subgoaling and depth-first search — and use different search methods for different problem spaces within the same problem [Rosenbloom et al., 1991, p. 310].

TABLE 1.3
Examples of SOAR's Task Achievements

Tasks	Examples
Search based	Broad variety of search methods; hill-climbing and depth-first search (singly and combined); operator subgoaling and depth-first search (singly and combined); range of search methods appropriate for range of problem spaces.
Knowledge based	R1-SOAR computer configuration system; the Cypress-SOAR design system; the Neomycin SOAR medical diagnosis system.
Learning	Learning from success; learning from failure; transfer of learned knowledge in trials and across problems; learning from a variety of sources.

Source: Rosenbloom, P. S., Laird, J. E., Newell, A. and McCarl, R. (1991). A preliminary analysis of the SOAR architecture as a basis for general intelligence. *Artificial Intelligence*, 47, 289–325.

SOAR's achievements with knowledge-based tasks are indicated in the following section.

Several knowledge-based tasks have been implemented in SOAR, including the R1-SOAR computer configuration system (Rosenbloom et al., 1987), the Cypress-SOAR and Designer-SOAR algorithm design systems (Steier, 1987; Steier and Newell, 1988), the Neomycin-SOAR medical diagnosis system (Washington and Rosenbloom, 1988), and the Merl-SOAR job-shop scheduling system (Hsu, Prietula, and Steier, 1988) [Rosenbloom et al., 1991, pp. 310–311].

SOAR's achievements with learning tasks are discussed in the following section.

The architecture directly supports a form of experiential learning in which chunking compiles goal-level problem solving into memory-level productions. Execution of the productions should have the same effect as the problem solving would have had, just more quickly. The varieties of subgoals for which chunks are learned lead to varieties in types of productions learned: problem space creation and selection; state creation and selection; and operator creation, selection, and execution. An alternative classification for this same set of behaviors is that it covers procedural, episodic and declarative knowledge [Rosenbloom, Newell, and Laird, 1990]. The variations in goal outcomes lead to both learning from success and learning from failure. The ability to learn about all subgoal results leads to learning about important intermediate results, in addition to learning about goal success and failure. The implicit generalization of chunks leads to transfer of learned knowledge to other subtasks within the same problem (within-trial transfer), other instances of the same problems (across-trial transfer), and other problems (across-task transfer). Variations in the types of problems performed in SOAR lead to chunking in knowledge-based tasks, search-based, and robotic tasks. Variations in sources of knowledge lead to learning from both internal and external knowledge sources. A summary of many of the types of learning that have so far been demonstrated in SOAR can be found in [Steier et al., 1987; Rosenbloom et al., 1991, p. 311].

SOAR: Source of Its Power

The reasons for SOAR's effectiveness and efficiency are discussed in the following section (Table 1.4).

SOAR's power and flexibility arise from at least four identifiable sources. The first source of power is the universality of the architecture. While it may seem that this should go without saying, it is in fact a crucial factor, and thus important to mention explicitly. Universality provides the primitive capability to perform any computable

TABLE 1.4

Sources of SOAR's Power and Flexibility

    I. Universality of its architecture
   II. Uniformity of its architecture
       A. Single type of memory structure
       B. Single type of task representation: problem spaces
       C. Single type of decision procedure
  III. Specific mechanisms built into its architecture
       A. Production memory
       B. Working memory
       C. Decision procedures and controls
       D. Subgoals
       E. Problem spaces
       F. Chunking
       G. Perceptual motor system
  IV. The coordination of methods and mechanisms within a unified system
       A. The combining of weak methods and learning mechanisms
       B. The combining of strong methods (knowledge) and weak methods (search)

---

task, but does not by itself explain why SOAR is more appropriate than any other universal architecture for knowledge-based, search-based, learning, and robotic tasks.

The second source of power is the uniformity of the architecture. Having only one type of long-term memory structure allows a single, relatively simple, learning mechanism to behave as a general learning mechanism. Having only one type of task representation (problem spaces) allows SOAR to move continuously from one extreme of brute-force search to the other extreme of knowledge-intensive (or procedural) behavior without having to make any representational decisions. Having only one type of decision procedure allows a single, relatively simple, subgoal mechanism to generate all of the types of subgoals needed by the system.

The traditional downside of uniformity is weakness and inefficiency. If instead the system were built up as a set of specialized modules or agents, as proposed in [Fodor, 1983; Minsky, 1986], then each of the modules could be optimized for its own narrow task. Our approach to this issue in SOAR has been to go strongly with uniformity — for all of the benefits listed above — but to achieve efficiency (power) through the addition of knowledge. This knowledge can either be added by hand (programming) or by chunking.

The third source of power is the specific mechanisms incorporated into the architecture. The production memory provides pattern-directed access to large amounts of knowledge; provides the ability to use strong problem solving methods; and provides a memory structure with a small-grained modularity. The working memory allows global access to processing state. The decision procedure provides an open control loop that can react immediately to new situations and knowledge; contributes to the modularity of the memory by allowing access to proceed in an uncontrolled fashion (conflict resolution was a major source of nonmodularity in earlier production systems); provides a flexible control language (preferences); and provides a notion of impasse that is used as the basis for the generation of subgoals. Subgoals focus the system's resources on situations where the accessible knowledge is inadequate; and allow flexible meta-level processing. Problem spaces separate control from action, allowing them (control and action) to be reasoned about independently; provide a constrained context within which the search for a desired state can occur; provide the ability to use weak problem solving methods; and provide for straightforward responses to uncertainty and error (search and backtracking). Chunking acquires long-term knowledge from experience; compiles interpreted procedures into non-interpreted ones; and provides generalization and transfer. The perceptual-motor system provides the ability to observe and affect the external world in parallel with the cognitive activity.

The fourth source of power is the interaction effects that result from the integration of all of the capabilities within a single system. The most compelling results generated so far come about from these interactions. One example comes from the mixture of weak methods, strong methods, and learning that is found in systems like R1-SOAR. Strong methods are based on having knowledge about what to do at each step. Because strong methods tend to be efficient and to produce high-quality solutions, they should be used whenever possible. Weak methods are based on searching to make up for lack of knowledge about what should be done. Such methods contribute robustness and scope by providing the system with a fall-back approach for situations in which the available strong methods do not work. Learning results in the addition of knowledge, turning weak methods into strong ones. For example, in R1-SOAR it was demonstrated how computer configuration could be cast as a search problem, how strong methods (knowledge) could be used to reduce search, how weak methods (subgoals and search) could be used to make up for a lack of knowledge, and how learning could add knowledge as the result of search.

Another interesting interaction effect comes from work on abstraction planning, in which a difficult problem is solved by first learning a plan for an abstract version of the problem, and then using the abstract plan to aid in finding a plan to solve the full problem (Newell & Simon, 1972; Sacerdoti, 1974; Unruh, Rosenbloom, & Laird, 1987; Unruh & Rosenbloom, 1989). Chunking helps the abstraction planning process by recording the abstract plan as a set of operator-selection production, and by acquiring other productions that reduce the amount of search required in generating a plan. Abstraction helps the learning process by allowing chunks to be learned more quickly — abstract searches tend to be shorter than normal ones. Abstraction also helps learning by enabling chunks to be more general than they would otherwise be — the chunks ignore the details that were abstracted away — thus allowing more transfer and potentially decreasing the cost of matching the chunks (because there are now fewer conditions) [italics added] [Rosenbloom et al., 1991, pp. 313–314].

SOAR: Scope and Limits

Rosenbloom and colleagues (1991) evaluate SOAR's progress and prospects in the following detailed discussion.

The original work on SOAR demonstrated its capabilities as a general problem solver that could use any of the weak methods when appropriate, across a wide range of tasks. Later we came to understand how to use SOAR as the basis for knowledge-based systems, and how to incorporate appropriate learning and perceptual-motor capabilities into the architecture. These developments increased SOAR's scope considerably beyond its origins as a weak-method problem solver. Our ultimate goal has always been to develop the system to the point where its scope includes everything required of a general intelligence. In this section we examine how far SOAR has come from its relatively limited initial demonstrations towards its relatively unlimited goal. This discussion is divided up according to the major components of the SOAR architecture, . . . memory, decisions, goals, learning, and perception and motor control.

Level 1: Memory

The scope of SOAR's memory level can be evaluated in terms of the amount of knowledge that can be stored, the types of knowledge that can be represented, and the organization of the knowledge.

Amount of knowledge. Using current technology, SOAR's production memory can support the storage of thousands of independent chunks of knowledge. The size is primarily limited by the cost of processing larger numbers of productions. Faster machines, improved match algorithms and parallel implementations [Gupta & Tambe, 1988; Tambe, Acharya, & Gupta, 1989; Tambe, Kalp, Gupta, Forgy, Milnes, & Newell, 1988] may raise this effective limit by several orders of magnitude over the next several years.
Types of knowledge. The representation of procedural and propositional declarative knowledge is well developed in SOAR. However, we don't have well worked-out approaches to many other knowledge representation problems, such as the representation of quantified, uncertain, temporal, and episodic knowledge. The critical question is whether architectural support is required to adequately represent these types of knowledge, or whether such knowledge can be adequately treated as additional objects and/or attributes. Preliminary work on quantified [Polk & Newell, 1988] and episodic [Rosenbloom, Newell, & Laird, 1990] knowledge is looking promising.
Memory organization. An issue that often gets raised with respect to the organization of SOAR's memory, and with respect to the organization of production memories in general, is the apparent lack of higher-order memory organization. There are no scripts [Schank & Ableson, 1977], frames [Minsky,

1975], or schemas [Bartlett, 1932] to tie fragments of related memory together. Nor are there any obvious hierarchical structures which limit what sets of knowledge will be retrieved at any point in time. However, SOAR's memory does have an organization, which is derived from the structure of productions, objects, and working memory (especially the context hierarchy).

What corresponds to a schema in SOAR is an object, or a structured collection of objects. Such a structure can be stored entirely in the actions of a single production, or it can be stored in a piecemeal fashion across multiple productions. If multiple productions are used, the schema as a unit only comes into existence when the pieces are all retrieved contemporaneously into working memory. The advantage of this approach is that it allows novel schemas to be created from fragments of separately learned ones. The disadvantage is that it may not be possible to determine whether a set of fragments all originated from a single schema.

What corresponds to a hierarchy of retrieval contexts in SOAR are the production conditions. Each combination of conditions implicitly defines a retrieval context, with a hierarchical structure induced by the subset relationship among the combinations. The contents of working memory determines which retrieval contexts are currently in force. For example, problem spaces are used extensively as retrieval contexts. Whenever there is a problem solving context that has a particular problem space selected within it, productions that test for other problem space names are not eligible to fire in that context. This approach has worked quite well for procedural knowledge, where it is clear when the knowledge is needed. We have just begun to work on appropriate organizational schemes for episodic and declarative knowledge, where it is much less clear when the knowledge should be retrieved. Our initial approach has been based on the incremental construction, via chunking, of multi-production discrimination networks [Rosenbloom, Laird, & Newell, 1988; Rosenbloom, Newell, & Laird, 1990]. Though this work is too premature for a thorough evaluation in the context of SOAR, the effectiveness of discrimination networks in systems like Epam [Feigenbaum & Simon, 1984] and Cyrus [Kolodner, 1983b] bodes well.

Level 2: Decisions

The scope of SOAR's decision level can be evaluated in terms of its speed, the knowledge brought to bear, and the language of control.

Speed. SOAR currently runs approximately 10 decisions/second on current workstations such as a Sun4/280. This is adequate for most of the types of tasks we currently implement, but it is too slow for tasks requiring large amounts of search or very large knowledge bases (the number of decisions per second would even get smaller than it is now). The principle bottleneck is the speed of memory access, which is a function of two factors: the cost of processing individually expensive productions [the *expensive chunks* problem) [Tambe & Newell, 1988], and the cost of processing a large number of productions (the *average growth effect* problem) [Tambe, 1988]. We now have a solution to the problem of expensive chunks which can guarantee that all productions will be cheap — the match cost of a production is at worst linear in the number of conditions [Tambe & Rosenbloom, 1989] — and are working on other potential solutions. Parallelism looks to be an effective solution to the average growth effect problem [Tambe, 1988].

Bringing knowledge to bear. Iterated, parallel, indexed access to the contents of long-term memory has proven to be an effective means of bringing knowledge to bear on the decision process. The limited power provided by this process is offset by the ability to use subgoals when the accessible knowledge is inadequate. The issue of devising good access paths for episodic and declarative knowledge is also relevant here.

Control language. Preferences have proven to be a flexible means of specifying a partial order among contending objects. However, we cannot yet state with certainty that the set of preference types embodied in SOAR is complete with respect to all the types of information which ultimately may need to be communicated to the decision procedure.

Level 3: Goals

The scope of SOAR's goal level can be evaluated in terms of the types of goals that can be generated and the types of problem solving that can be performed in goals. SOAR's subgoaling mechanism has been demonstrated to be able to create subgoals for all of the types of difficulties that can arise in problem solving in problem spaces (Laird, 1986). This leaves three areas open. The first area is how top-level goals are generated; that is, how the top level task is picked. Currently this is done by the programmer, but a general intelligence must clearly have grounds — that is, motivations — for selecting tasks on its own. The second area is how goal interactions are handled. Goal interactions show up in SOAR as operator interactions, and are normally dealt with by adding explicit knowledge to avoid them, or by backtracking (with learning) when they happen. It is not yet clear the extent to which SOAR could easily make use of more sophisticated approaches, such as non-linear planning (Chapman, 1987). The third area is the sufficiency of impasse-driven subgoaling as a means for determining when meta-level processing is needed. Two of the activities that might fall under this area are goal tests and monitoring. Both of these activities can be performed at the memory or decision level, but when they are complicated activities it may be necessary to perform them by problem solving at the goal level. Either activity can be called for explicitly by selecting a "monitor" or "goal-test" operator, which can then lead to the generation of a subgoal. However, goals for these tasks do not arise automatically, without deliberations. Should they? It is not completely clear.

The scope of the problem solving that can be performed in goals can itself be evaluated in terms of whether problem spaces cover all of the types of performance required, the limits on the ability of subgoal-based problem solving to access and modify aspects of the system, and whether parallelism is possible. These points are addressed in the next three paragraphs.

Problem space scope. Problem spaces are a very general performance model. They have been hypothesized to underlie all human, symbolic, goal-oriented behavior [Newell, 1980]. The breadth of tasks that have so far been represented in problem spaces over the whole field of AI attests to this generality. One way of pushing this evaluation further is to ask how well problem spaces account for the types of problem solving performed by two of the principal competing paradigms: planning [Chapman, 1987] and case-based reasoning [Kolodner, 1988]. Both of these paradigms involve the creation (or retrieval) and use of a data structure that represents a sequence of actions. In planning, the data structure represents the sequence of actions that the system expects to use for the current problem. In case-based reasoning, the data structure represents the sequence of actions used on some previous, presumably related, problem. In both, the data structure is used to decide what sequence of actions to perform in the current problem. SOAR straightforwardly performs procedural analogues of these two processes. When it performs a look ahead search to determine what operator to apply to a particular state, it acquires (by chunking) a set of search control productions which collectively tell it which operator should be applied to each subsequent state. This set of chunks forms a procedural plan for the current problem. When a search control chunk transfers between tasks, a form of procedural case-based reasoning is occurring.

Simple forms of declarative planning and case-based reasoning have also been demonstrated in SOAR in the context of an expert system that designs floor systems (Reich, 1988). When this system discovers, via look ahead search, a sequence of operators that achieves a goal, it creates a declarative structure representing the sequence and returns it as a subgoal result (plan creation). This plan can then be used interpretively to guide performance on the immediate problem (plan following). The plan can also be retrieved during later problems and used to guide the selection of operators (case-based reasoning). This research does not demonstrate the variety of operations one could conceivably use to modify a partial or complete plan, but it does demonstrate the basics.

Meta-level access. Subgoal-based problem solving has access to all of the information in working memory — including the goal stack, problem spaces, states, operators, preferences, and other facts that have been retrieved or generated — plus any of the other knowledge in long-term memory that it can access. It does not have direct access to the productions, or to any of the data structures internal to the architecture. Nonetheless, it should be able to indirectly examine the contents of any productions that were acquired by chunking, which in the long run should be just about all of them. The idea is to reconstruct the contents of the production by going down into a subgoal and retracing the problem solving that was done when the chunk was learned. In this way it should be possible to determine what knowledge the production cached. This idea has not yet been explicitly demonstrated in SOAR, but research on the recovery from incorrect knowledge has used a closely related approach [Laird, 1988].

The effects of problem solving are limited to the addition of information to working memory. Detection of working memory elements is accomplished by a garbage collector provided by the architecture. Productions are added by chunking, rather than by problem solving, and are never deleted by the system. The limitation on production creation — that it only occurs via chunking — is dealt with by varying the nature of the problem solving over which chunking occurs [Rosenbloom, Newell, and Laird, 1990]. The limitation on production deletion is dealt with by learning new productions which overcome the effects of old ones [Laird, 1988].

Parallelism. Two principal sources of parallelism in SOAR are at the memory level: production match and execution. On each cycle of elaboration, all productions are matched in parallel to the working memory, and then all of the successful instantiations are executed in parallel. This lets tasks that can be performed at the memory level proceed in parallel, but not so for decision-level and goal-level tasks.

Another principal source of parallelism is provided by the motor systems. All motor systems behave in parallel with respect to each other, and with respect to the cognitive system. This enables one form of task-level parallelism in which non-interfering external tasks can be performed in parallel. To enable further research on task-level parallelism we have added the experimental ability to simultaneously select multiple problem space operators within a single problem solving context. Each of these operators can then proceed to execute in parallel, yielding parallel subgoals, and ultimately an entire tree of problem solving contexts in which all of the branches are being processed in parallel. We do not yet have enough experience with this capability to evaluate its scope and limits.

Despite all of these forms of parallelism embodied in SOAR, most implementations of the architecture have been on serial machines, with the parallelism being simulated. However, there is an active research effort to implement SOAR on parallel computers. A parallelized version of the production match has been successfully implemented on an Encore Multimax, which has a small number (2–20) of large-grained processors [Tambe et al., 1988], and unsuccessfully implemented on a Connection Machine [Hillis, 1985], which has a large number (16K–64K) of small-grained processors [Flynn, 1988]. The Connection Machine implementation failed primarily because a complete parallelization of the current match algorithm can lead to exponential space requirements. Research on restricted match algorithms may fix this problem in the future. Work is also in progress toward implementing SOAR on message-passing computers [Tambe, Acharya, and Gupta, 1989].

Learning. In [Steier et al., (1987)] we broke down the problem of evaluating the scope of SOAR's learning capabilities into four parts: when can the architecture learn; from what can the architecture learn; what can the architecture learn; and when can the architecture apply learned knowledge.

One important additional issue is whether SOAR acquires knowledge that is at the appropriate level of generalization or specialization. Chunking provides a level of generality that is determined by a combination of the representation used and the problem solving performed. Under varying circumstances, this can lead to both overgeneralization [Laird, Rosenbloom, and Newell, 1986] and overspecialization. The acquisition of overgeneral knowledge implies that the system must be able to recover from any errors caused by its use. One solution to this problem that has been implemented in SOAR involves detecting that a performance error has occurred, determining what should have been done instead, and acquiring a new chunk which leads to correct performance in the future [Laird, 1988]. This is accomplished without examining or modifying the overgeneral production; instead it goes back down into the subgoals for which the overgeneral productions were learned.

One way to deal with overspecialization is to patch the resulting knowledge gaps with additional knowledge. This is what SOAR does constantly — if a production is overspecialized, it doesn't fire in circumstances when it should, causing an impasse to occur, and providing the opportunity to learn an additional chunk that covers the missing case (and possibly other cases). Another way to deal with overspecialized knowledge is to work towards acquiring more general productions. A standard approach is to induce general rules from a sequence of positive and negative examples [Mitchell, 1982; Quinlan, 1986]. This form of generalization must occur in SOAR by search in problem spaces, and though there has been some initial work on doing this [Rosenbloom, 1988; Saul, 1984], we have not yet provided SOAR with a set of problem spaces that will allow it to generate appropriate generalizations from a variety of sets of examples. So, SOAR cannot yet be described as a system of choice for doing induction from multiple examples. On the other hand, SOAR does generalize quite naturally and effectively when abstraction occurs [Unruh & Rosenbloom, 1989]. The learned rules reflect whatever abstraction was made during problem solving.

Learning behaviors that have not yet been attempted in SOAR include the construction of a model of the environment from experimentation in it [Rajamoney, DeJong, & Faltings, 1985], scientific discovery and theory formation [Langley, Simon, Bradshaw, & Zytkow, 1987], and conceptual clustering [Fisher & Langley, 1985].

Perception and motor control. The scope of SOAR's perception and motor control can be evaluated in terms of both its low-level I/O [input-output] mechanisms and its high-level language capabilities. Both of these capabilities are quite new, so the evaluation must be even more tentative than for the preceding components.

At the low-level, SOAR can be hooked up to multiple perceptual modalities (and multiple fields within each modality) and can control multiple effectors. The critical low-level aspects of perception and motor control are currently done in a standard procedural language outside of the cognitive system. The resulting system appears to be an effective testbed for research on high-level aspects of perception and motor-control. It also appears to be an effective testbed for research on the interactions of perception and motor control with other cognitive capabilities, such as memory, problem solving, and learning. However, it does finesse many of the hard issues in perception and motor control, such as selective attention, shape determination, object identification, and temporal coordination. Work is actively in progress on selective attention [Weismeyer, 1988].

At the high end of I/O capabilities is the processing of natural language. An early attempt to implement a semantic grammar parser in SOAR was only a limited success [Powell, 1984]. It worked, but it did not appear to be the right long-term solution to language understanding in SOAR. More recent work on NL-SOAR has focussed on the incremental construction of a model of the situation by applying comprehension operators to each incoming word [Lewis, Newell, & Polk, 1989]. Comprehension operators iteratively augment and refine the situation model, setting up expectations for the part of the utterance still to be seen, and satisfying earlier expectations. As a side effect of constructing the situation model, an utterance model is constructed to represent the linguistic structure of the sentence. This approach to language under-standing has been successfully applied to acquiring task-specific problem spaces for three immediate reasoning tasks: relational reasoning [Johnson-Laird, 1988], categorical syllogisms, and sentence verification [Clark & Chase, 1972]. It has also been used to process the input for these tasks as they are performed. Though NL-SOAR is still far from providing a general linguistic capability, the approach has proven promising [italics added] [Rosenbloom et al., 1991, pp. 314–321].

Commentary

SOAR is, at once, an advanced artificial intelligence system directed toward the emulation of human cognition, a theoretical and research tool for testing and integrating the data of experimental cognitive psychology, an empirical research program with foundations resting on the basic concepts contained on the physical symbol system hypothesis, a methodology that draws upon the concepts, techniques, and data of cognitive science, and, ultimately, a unified theory of human and artificial cognition.

SOAR's central value is that it provides theoretical and research instrumentation for the long-term conceptual integration of the numerous diverse findings of experimental studies in cognitive psychology and artificial intelligence.

COGNITIVE PSYCHOLOGY: OBJECTIVES, SOURCES, AND APPROACHES

Objectives

The major objectives of cognitive psychology are to render a descriptive, structural, and dynamic account of human intelligence cast in the form of mathematical equations that represent verified knowledge of specific cognitive mechanisms and their interlocking functions.

Sources

The major sources of cognitive psychology are the psychological sciences, the computational sciences, the neural sciences, the linguistic sciences, and the philosophical sciences.

Approaches

The major approaches of cognitive psychology include descriptive accounts of environmental information and conjectures about the cognitive mechanisms that process that information (ecological psychology), controlled laboratory studies of imputed cognitive mechanisms and their associated empirical data (experimental psychology), formal mathematical representations of cognitive variables, relations, functions, and mechanisms (mathematical psychology), and computer simulations of the theoretical structures and processes of cognition (computational psychology). Table 1.5 presents an organized summary of the major approaches to cognitive psychology.

TABLE 1.5

Major Approaches to Cognitive Psychology

   I. Data-focused approaches
      A. Ecological psychology
      B. Experimental psychology
  II. Theory-focused approaches
      A. Mathematical psychology
      B. Computational psychology
 III. Contributions of the approaches
      A. Ecological psychology
         1. Analysis of specific environments
         2. Processes of adaptation to environment
      B. Experimental psychology
         1. Experimentally obtained data in laboratory situations
         2. Cognitive mechanisms inferred from controlled experimentation
      C. Mathematical psychology
         1. Mathematical equations define cognitive mechanisms
         2. Mathematical equations imply theoretical deductions and experimentally testable predictions concerning cognitive mechanisms
      D. Computational psychology
         1. Computational simulations test theories that are too complex to test experimentally
         2. Computational simulations provide theoretical accounts that meet the criterion of sufficiency

---

2

Reasoning

A central research paradigm in cognitive science consists of the collection of protocols of subjects thinking aloud as they solve problems, the construction of computational models of the problem-solving process, and control experimentation designed to test predictions derived from the models. This research paradigm is deployed by Rips (1989) in a lucid study of deductive inference processes. In this section, Rips' (1989) research will be described, and, then, a general commentary will be presented.

GENERAL DESCRIPTION OF KNIGHT-KNAVE PROBLEMS

Rips' (1989) research concerns reasoning with knight-knave problems.

Knight-knave puzzles begin like this: Suppose there is an island where there are just two sorts of inhabitants — knights who always tell the truth and knaves who always lie. Nothing distinguishes knights and knaves but their lying or truth-telling propensity. You overhear a conversation between two or more inhabitants, and on the basis of their conversation, you must decide which of the individuals are knights and which are knaves. Smullyan (1978) is a rich source of these puzzles, of which the following is an example:

We have three inhabitants, A, B, and C, each of whom is a knight or a knave. Two people are said to be of the same type if they are both knights or both knaves. A and B make the following statements:

A: B is a knave.
B: A and C are of the same type. What is C? [Smullyan, 1978, p. 22]

Although the answer isn't obvious, a little thought yields the solution. To get started, suppose that A is a knight. Since what he says is true, B would then be a knave. But if B is a knave, he is lying, which means that A and C are not of the same type. We're assuming that A is a knight: so on this assumption, C must be a knave. But what if A is a knave rather than a knight? Well, in that case, A's statement is false, and hence B is a knight. This makes A and C of the same type, which means that C is a knave. So no matter whether we take A to be a knight or a knave, C will be a knave, and this must be the answer to the puzzle [Rips, 1989, pp. 85–86].

PROTOCOL OF DEDUCTION WITH A KNIGHT-KNAVE PROBLEM

Table 2.1 presents the protocol of a subject thinking out loud as she reasoned with a knight-knave problem. Rips (1989) provides the following commentary on the protocol:

TABLE 2.1
Protocol from Subject 3 on Knight-Knave Problem (1)

---

a. Well, the *type* introduction, that's a little confusing.
b. If A is a knight, then B has to be lying.
c. So A and C are of, are not of the same type.
d. That would mean that B and C are knaves.
e. So that's one possibility.
f. If A is a knave, then B is a knight, and A and C are both knaves.
g. Now I've forgotten my first possibility.
h. If A is a knight, then B ...* if A is a knight, B is a knave and C is a knave.
i. So my first possibility is C is a knave.
j. Second possibility is if A is a knave ... Wait a minute...
k. If A is a knight, no, if A is a knight, then C is a knave.
l. Uh, if A is a knave ..., then C is a knave.
m. So either way, C is a knave.

---

*Ellipses indicate pauses
Source: Rips, L. J. (1989). The psychology of knights and knaves. *Cognition, 31,* 85–116. Reprinted with the permission of Elsevier Science Publishers, B.V., and the author.

[Table 2.1] presents a complete transcript from one of the subjects, a college freshman, who was working on Problem (1). In general, her line of attack follows the pattern we gave earlier. The subject begins by assuming that person A is a knight. Since what A says is true on this assumption and since A says that B is a knave, the subject infers that B is lying (line b). B's statement that A and C are of the same type must therefore be false. But by assumption, A is a knight, and thus C must be a knave. So by line d of [Table 2.1] the subject is able to conclude that B and C are knaves if A is a knight, and she calls this her "first possibility." She then turns to the second possibility: that A is a knave. This means that B is a knight, so that A and C are of the same type, namely knaves. In line g, though, the subject runs into a temporary problem in that she has forgotten C's "type" under the first possibility. This was not uncommon in the experiment, since subjects were not able to write down their intermediate results. In line h and i, she goes back to re-compute the first part of her solution, and in line j begins again on the second part. But before she develops the latter possibility, she apparently has some second thoughts about the first. Finally, she reminds herself of the implications of the second possibility, and in line m correctly concludes that in either possibility C is a knave.

The protocol in [Table 2.1] is one of the most articulate solutions in our sample, but some of the properties of this answer are representative. First, the subjects attempted to solve the problems by considering specific assumptions. In order to solve Problem (1), the subject of [Table 2.1] tries to determine whether the speakers, A and B, are knights or knaves, since she can then use the truth or falsity of their statements to determine whether C is a knight or knave. However, the problem doesn't identify A or B directly, and so it is not clear how to get a start on the answer. The subject's strategy is to make an assumption or supposition about A's status (that A is a knight) and see what this supposition implies about C. Once she has determined that in this case C is a knave, she can back up and make the opposite assumption that A is a knave. The transcripts contain many similar instances of assumption making.

Second, subjects tended to work forward from their assumptions about the lying or truth-telling of the speakers to implications for the question. They usually didn't make assumptions about the answer and work backward to see if they are implied or contradicted by the given information, even though this strategy is equally logical. For example, another way to solve (1) is to show that the assumption that C is a knight leads to a contradiction so that (by reductio ad absurdum) C must be a knave. There is no evidence in the transcripts that the subjects attempted such a strategy on this problem. In other problems there are hints of backward reasoning, but they are rare. Along the same lines, subjects ordinarily use the fact that a particular individual is a knight or knave to establish the truth or falsity of what that individual says, rather than going from the truth or falsity of a statement to the status of the speaker. We should exercise caution here, however, since lack of evidence for backward reasoning may be due to difficulties subjects have in describing it in the thinking-aloud context.

Finally, subjects usually had the logical resources they needed to solve the puzzles, but sometimes forgot assumptions, confused intermediate results, or gave up too soon. For example, one of the subjects began attack on Puzzle (1) like this:

A says B is a knave, that's either true or false. Keeping that in mind, B says that A and C are of the same type. So if A is telling the truth, C is also of A's type, which is truth-telling-knights — A and C are both knights if B is telling the truth. If B is telling the truth and A is telling the truth, well, something, neither, not both of them can be right, because either A is correct about B's being a knave, or . . . wait, this is getting confusing.

This subject tries to consider all possible ways in which A and B could be assigned to the knight and knave categories and begins to get lost in the process. There are cases in which subjects do run up against more clearly logical troubles, but most of the subjects' difficulties involved conceptual bookkeeping rather than narrowly logical deficiencies [Rips, 1989, pp. 87–89].

COMPUTATIONAL MODEL OF KNIGHT-KNAVE PROBLEMS

Rips (1989) summarizes the theoretical background for the development of a computational model of knight-knave problems in the following terms.

The proposed model derives from a prior theory of human propositional reasoning (Rips, 1983, 1984), which is based on the idea that *people deal with deduction problems by applying mental-deduction rules, like those of formal natural-deduction systems* (Gentzen, 1969; Jaskowski, 1934). The theory is therefore similar to earlier psychological proposals by Braine (1978) and Osherson (1974–1976), which also rely on natural-deduction frameworks. *The deduction rules apply to information stored in working memory and perform inferences that follow from it.* A typical deduction rule, for example, is And Elimination, which applies to a working-memory sentence of the form p AND q and produces the two sentences p and q, stated separately. *The deduction rules implement elementary inference principles; but by stringing these inferences together, people can create more complex mental derivations or proofs that show how a remote conclusion follows from its premises. The theory predicts subjects' performance on a deduction problem in terms of the length of the required derivation and the availability of the rules: The shorter the derivation and the more available the rules that generate it, the faster and more accurate subjects should be* [italics added] [Rips, 1989, p. 90].

Rips (1989) gives the following account of the conceptual and technical features of the computational model.

The model for the knight-knave problems is a version of the natural deduction system with a few additional rules to handle the special constraints of the task. To represent the new rules, we use the expressions knight (x) to mean that x is a knight, Knave (x) to mean x is a knave, and says (x,p) to mean that person x uttered the sentence p. So, for example, says (A, knave (B)) represents the proposition that A said B is a knave. In these terms, the four new rules are the ones in [Table 2.2]. The first allows us to infer that p is true if a knight said it; the second, that p is false if a knave said it; the third, that someone who is not a knave is a knight; and the fourth, that someone who is not a knight is a knave. Other rules could be obtained from the problem definition: for example, it is also true that says (x, p) and NOT p entail knave (x). But, as mentioned earlier, these inference patterns were not very common in the protocols and were therefore not included in the model. The remaining rules are all simple inferences from propositional logic, which depend on more complex logic; however, these propositional rules are sufficient to create problems that span a wide range of difficulty and enable us to test the model's basic features.

TABLE 2.2
Knight-Knave Rules Used in Constructing
Problems for Experiments 1 and 2

Rule 1:	*says (x,p)* and *knight (x)* entail *p*.
Rule 2:	*says (x,p)* and *knave (x)* entail *NOT p*.
Rule 3:	*NOT knave (x)* entails *knight (x)*.
Rule 4:	*NOT knight (x)* entails *knave (x)*.

Source: Rips, L. J. (1989). The psychology of knights and knaves. *Cognition, 31*, 85–116. Reprinted with the permission of Elsevier Science Publishers, B.V., and the author.

The model exists as a PROLOG program that accepts sentences of the form just described and makes assumptions and draws inferences about knight/knave identity.

Readers who know PROLOG may find this use of the language odd, since the model is in effect a theorem prover built on top of a language that contains its own theorem-proving mechanism (see, e.g., Clocksin and Mellish, 1981). Why not take advantage of PROLOG's native logical abilities to solve the problems directly? The answer is that the model attempts to specify the cognitive processes of human novices, and these processes are probably far removed from PROLOG's own sophisticated resolution methods. For this reason, PROLOG functions here simply as a convenient programming language, just as if we had used LISP [list programming]. Using a logic-based programming language to construct a model of human reasoning is no stranger than the fact that AI reasoning systems (including PROLOG, for that matter) run on hardware that has its own logic circuitry.

The program consists of a simple production system linked to representations in working memory. These representations include the assumed and deduced sentences, together with the dependency relations among them. In the latter respect, the model resembles the AI reasoning systems of Stallman and Sussman (1977) and Doyle (1980). The program begins by storing the (logical form of the) sentences in the problem and extracting from them the names of the individuals (e.g., A, B, and C). It then assumes that the first-mentioned individually — usually, A — is a knight and draws as many inferences as it can from this assumption and the given sentences. The program obtains the inferences by applying its rule to the stored sentences, initially in the order given in [Table 2.3]. If the program detects a pair of contradictory sentences (e.g., knight (B) and knave (B)) during this process, it immediately abandons its assumption that A is a knight and assumes instead that A is a knave. However, if the new set of inferences is consistent, it proceeds to assume that the second mentioned individual is a knight. After each step, the program revises the ordering of its rules so that rules that have successfully been applied will be tried first on the next round. The program continues in this way until it has found all consistent sets of assumptions about the knight/knave status of the individuals. Finally, it reports that an individual x is a knight if knight (x) appears in all of the consistent sets, that x is a knave if knave (x) appears in all of the consistent sets, and that x's identity is undetermined in all other cases [Rips, 1989, pp. 90–91].

TABLE 2.3

Propositional Rules in Constructing
Problems for Experiments 1 and 2

Rule 5 (AND Elimination):	*p AND q* entails *p,q.*
Rule 6 (Modus Ponens):	*IF p THEN q* and *p* entail *q.*
Rule 7 (Demorgan-1):	*NOT (p OR q)* entails *NOT p AND NOT q.*
Rule 8 (Demorgan-2):	*NOT (p AND q)* entails *NOT p OR NOT q.*
Rule 9 (Disjunctive Syllogism-1):	*p OR q* and *NOT p* entail *q.*
	p OR q and *NOT q* entail *p.*
Rule 10 (Disjunctive Syllogism-2):	*NOT p OR q* and *p* entail *q.*
	p OR NOT q and *q* entail *p.*
Rule 11 (Double Negation Elimination):	*NOT NOT p* entails *p.*

Source: Rips, L. J. (1989). The psychology of knights and knaves. *Cognition, 31*, 85–116. Reprinted with the permission of Elsevier Science Publishers, B.V., and the author.

Rips (1989) presents the following example of the problem-solving performance of the computational model.

As an example of the program's operation, let's consider how it would solve Problem (1). Since the program has no facility for parsing English sentences, the given information must be presented in logical form. The first given sentence is simply says (A, knave (B)). The second can be represented as says (B, knight (A) IF-AND-ONLY-IF knight (C)), since we can capture the notion of same type as a bi-conditional. The program stores these sentences in a node of its working memory. . . . None of the program's inference rules apply to these sentences directly. To make any headway, the program has to try out some assumptions, and the first assumption it makes is knight (A). This assumption and the inferences that follow from it are stored in a subordinate node of working memory in order to indicate their hypothetical status (see Rips, 1983). The new assumption, together with the first of the original sentences, triggers one of the program's knight-knave rules (Rule 1 of [Table 2.2]), which permits it to infer knave (B). This in turn yields NOT (knight (A) IF-AND-ONLY-IF knight (C)) by knight-knave Rule 2. The program then uses a propositional rule to deduce knave (C) from the negated bi-conditional and the assumption knight (A). At this point, no more inferences follow. The program briefly considers whether B might be a knight, but rejects this possibility immediately since it directly contradicts the conclusion that B is a knave. It then stores the assumption that B is a knave at a subordinate node in memory. Similarly, it rejects the possibility that C is a knight in favor of the assumption that C is a knave. The program has now found a consistent set of assumptions: A is a knight and B and X are knaves. However, it is not through, since it has yet to consider the possibility that A is a knave. It therefore backs up and explores the consequences of the assumption. From knave (A), the program can conclude that NOT (knave (B)) and hence knight (B), according to Rules 2 and 3. This implies knight (A) IF-AND-ONLY-IF knight (C) by Rule 1. One of the propositional rules recognizes that the bi-conditional and the assumption knave (A) yields the final conclusion knave (C). Thus, the only assumptions about B and C that are consistent with the possibility that A is a knave are that B is a knight and C is a knave. *This means the program has found two consistent sets of assumptions: Either A is a knight and B and C are knaves or B is a knight and A and C are knaves. Because the identity of A and B depends on the assumptions, the program describes them as uncertain. But it declares C a knave, since this is true in both sets. This solution follows in outline, the method used by the subject of* [Table 2.1] [italics added] [Rips, 1989, pp. 91–93].

EXPERIMENT ONE

Rationale

Rips (1989) programmed the inference rules of Table 2.1 and Table 2.2 in the computational model of knight-knave problems. Rips (1989) claims that these inference rules are the same ones that subjects would use in experimental tests of the model.

To test the model, we constructed a variety of knight-knave puzzles that could be solved by means of the knight-knave rules in [Table 2.2], together with the propositional rules of [Table 2.3]. Previous cognitive theories have claimed the propositional rules of the table as psychologically primitive. For example, Rules 5, 6, 9, and 11 appear in the theory of Braine, Reiser, and Rumain (1984); Rules 5, 7, 8, and 11 in Osherson (1975), and Rules 5, 6, 8, and 9 in Rips (1983). Rule 10 is the only one that has not appeared in previous models, but it seems an obvious corollary of Rule 9. *We claim that these rules are the elementary inference principles that subjects will rely on in solving the puzzles in our stimulus ensemble. We do not assume, however, that the [Table 2.3] rules necessarily exhaust the primitive inferences that subjects are able to draw.*
To derive predictions about the difficulty of the problems, we submitted them to the PROLOG program described earlier and counted the number of inference steps that the program needed to solve them. This inference-step measure serves as our main independent variable. However, the problems also varied in the number of knight or knave characters (either 2 or 3) and in the number of clauses in the problem statement. We therefore paired the problems so that the two items in each pair contained the same number of individuals and clauses, but differed in the number of steps in their solutions. *Our basic prediction, then, is that, within a given pair, the problem with a larger number of inferences will produce larger error rates* [italics added] [Rips, 1989, p. 94].

Method

Rips (1989) describes the experimental procedure and instruction to subjects as follows:

The subjects in this experiment received a group of knight-knave problems, and they decided for each person in a problem whether that person was a knight, a knave, or was undetermined. At the beginning of the experiment, we gave subjects a detailed introduction to the type of puzzle they would see. We illustrated the definitions of knight and knave with sentences that might be said by a knight (e.g., A says "2+2=4") or a knave (e.g., B says, "2+2=5"). A sample problem showed them how to mark their answer sheets, which listed each of the speakers alongside boxes labeled "knight," "knave," and "impossible to tell." We read these instructions to the subjects, while they followed along in their own booklets. We then gave subjects a packet containing 34 problems, one problem per page. (The problems appeared in a different random order for each subject.) They proceeded through the booklet, under instructions to work the problems in order and not to return to a problem once they had completed it. Although we recorded the approximate amount of time they spent on the task, the subjects worked at their own pace. Unlike the subjects of the pilot experiment, these subjects were able to write down any information they wished [Rips, 1989, p. 95].

The characteristics of the experimental problems are given in the following account:

The experimental problems consisted of a list of speakers (A, B, and C) and their utterances, and they required subjects to mark the type of each speaker or to mark "impossible to tell." Six of the problems had two speakers; the remaining 28 had three. The two-speaker problems contained three or four clauses, while the three-speaker problems contained four, five, or nine clauses. For these purposes, a clause is an elementary phrase such as B is a knave or I am not a knight. We counted clauses in terms of the underlying form of the sentence: so both A is a knave and B is a knave and A and B are knaves contain two clauses. A sentence such as All of us are knights counts as two clauses — i.e., knight(A) and knight(B) — in the context of a problem with two speakers and as three clauses in a three-speaker problem. As we mentioned, problems were paired in order to equate the number of speakers and clauses. As an example, Problems (2) and (3) formed one of the pairs of four clauses, three-speaker items:

(2) A says, "C is a knave."
     B says, "C is a knight."
     C says, "A is a knight and B is a knave."
(3) A says, "B is a knight."
     B says, "C is a knave or A is a knight."
     C says, "A is a knight."

For the [experimental] problems, the simulation program printed a complete derivation, according to the principles discussed in the preceding section. *We calculated the predicted difficulty of the problem as the number of assumed and inferred propositions that the program considered before reaching the correct answer. For example, the program needed 16 steps to solve Problem (2), and 20 steps for Problem (3). Hence we predict that subjects will make more mistakes on (3) than on (2)*[italics added] [Rips, 1989, pp. 95–96].

Results and Discussion

The major experimental findings are given in the following summary:

Solution rate was 20%, with range from 0% correct for the least successful subject to 84% correct for the most successful one. . . . The individual problems varied over a more modest interval: None of the subjects solved the most difficult problem and 35% solved the easiest one [Rips, 1989, p. 97].

The relation of these findings to the experimental predictions are interpreted by Rips (1989) as follows:

These data support the model's basic prediction concerning the relative difficulty of paired items. Subjects solved 24% of the problems that the model predicted to be easier, but 16% of the problems the model predicted to be difficult. This difference is significant when problem pairs serve as the unit of analysis. . . , and also when subjects serve as the unit. . . . In absolute terms, the difference is fairly small, but the low overall solution rate puts a cap on the size of the effect. Moreover, there is only a small theoretical difference in the number of steps that the two groups of problems require. The simulation used a mean of 19.3 steps in solving the simpler problems and 24.2 steps in solving the harder ones.

In sum, the findings are consistent with the basic prediction that subjects should score higher on puzzles with a smaller number of inference steps [italics added] [Rips, 1989, pp. 97–99].

EXPERIMENT TWO

Rationale

In experiment one, predictions derived from the natural deduction model concern subjects' error rate. In experiment two, predictions derived from the model focus on subjects' response time. Rips (1989) describes the rationale for experiment two in the following terms:

The goal of this experiment is to provide a more stringent test of the natural deduction model. In the first place, we try to show that the model is able to predict the amount of time subjects take to reach a correct solution. *The form of the prediction is analogous to what we have seen before: The more steps the model needs to find the answer to a problem, the longer subjects should take to get it right.* The response-time measure, however, motivated us to simplify the problems. Puzzles such as (1)–(4) would produce extremely long and variable times and would yield too few correct answers for analysis.

Second, we attempted to impose tighter control on the form of the problems in order to avoid the confoundings discussed in the previous section. To see how this can be done, consider the following puzzles:

(5)   A: "I am a knave and B is a knave."
      B: "I am a knight."

(6)   A: "I am a knave and B is a knave."
      B: "A is a knave."

(7)   A: "I am a knight and B is a knight."
      B: "A is a knave."

Notice that all three items have exactly the same surface and underlying form, differing only in the content of their clauses. In particular, the only connective in these problems, the *and* in the first sentence, is constant across (5)–(7). The problems also have the same answer, since in each of them A must be a knave and B a knight. Nevertheless, the model predicts Problem (7) to be more difficult than either (5) or (6). One reason for this is that in (5) and (6) the model quickly disposes of the (incorrect) possibility that A is a knight. For if A is a knight in these first two problems, then what A says is true, which is that he and B are knaves. But this means that A himself is a knave, contrary to assumption. By contrast, if the A of (7) is a knight, we're entitled to conclude from his statement only that he and B are knights. We must consult B's statement and realize that if B is a knight then A must be a knave, before we can rule out the possibility that A is a knight. Thus, (7) will require more steps in total than either (5) or (6). We take advantage of matched triples such as (5)–(7) in this experiment to eliminate irrelevant effects of problem working and response [italics added] [Rips, 1989, pp. 99–100].

Method

The experimental procedure and instructions to subjects are given in the following account:

Subjects in this study viewed the problems on a monitor and decided for each problem about the knight/knave status of its two characters. The subjects' instructions were similar to information about the trial sequence and the response apparatus. The subjects controlled a response panel that contained a single button at the left and three clustered buttons at the right. At the start of the trial, they were to have their left index finger on the left-hand button and their right index finger on the enter button of the three-button group. The monitor signaled the beginning of the trial with the word "START," and when the subjects were ready to begin, they pressed the left button. The screen cleared, and then presented the problem in the form shown in (5)–(7), with the prompt "A?" underneath. At this point, subjects decided on the identity of person A and pressed one of the outer two buttons at the right with their right index finger to indicate their answer. After they did so, they returned their finger to the middle and pressed the center button. The prompt "B?" appeared on the screen, and the subjects made one last button press in the same way to record their decision about person B. Finally, the monitor presented the subjects with feedback about the accuracy of their answer and the amount of time they had taken.

The instructions told subjects that some of the problems would be difficult and that they should be sure their decision was correct before responding. They were also told, "once you have found the right answer, don't delay in pressing the button. Respond to each problem as fast as you can without making any errors." . . . *A microcomputer randomized the problems in a new order for each subject, controlled the trial sequence, and recorded the button presses and response times* [italics added] [Rips, 1989, p. 101].

The characteristics of the experimental problems are given in the following summary:

We chose the problems from those formed by selecting all possible combinations of options in the following frame:

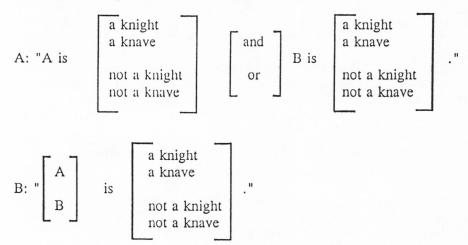

This procedure yields 256 potential problems. However, since NOT (knight(x)) is equivalent to knave(x) and NOT (knave(x)) to knight(x), we can think of this set as consisting of 32 problem groups, where the 8 problems within each group differ only in the presence of negatives. For example, Problems (9) and (10) are from the same group:

(9) A: "A is a knave and B is a knave."
     B: "B is a knight."
(10) A: "A is not a knight and B is a knave."
     B: "B is not a knave."

To summarize the sentences less awkwardly, we replaced the names with the pronoun I where it was appropriate. For example, instead of the sentence B: "B is a knight," subjects saw B: "I am a knight."

We submitted each of the problems to the natural-deduction program and chose 12 of the groups for this experiment on the basis of output. The sample problems in [Table 2.4] summarize the selection. Each of the sample problems in the table represents one problem group, as defined earlier. The rows of the table show that three groups of problems had A is a knight and B is a knight as the correct response; three had A is a knight and B is a knave; three had A is a knave and B is a knight; and three had A is a knave and B is a knave. The three groups within each row also had the same connective (and or or). *However, the groups differ in the number of inference steps that the model needed to solve them: The problems in the first two columns required relatively few steps (13.1 for column 1 and 13.0 for column 2) and those in the last column relatively many (16.4 steps).* In what follows, we refer to items in column 1 (which contain the sentence B: "I am a knight" or B: "I am not a knave") as the first type of small-step problems and to items in column 2 as the second type of small-step problems. Column 3 contains large-step problems. *Our prediction, then, is that response times should be longer and errors more frequent for the large-step problems within each row of the table* [italics added] [Rips, 1989, pp. 101–102].

The experimental method established criteria for the rejection of data from those subjects who might make an excessive number of errors in responding to the problems.

On the basis of the earlier study, we expected that many subjects would be unable to complete the test without making a large number of incorrect responses. *Since these trials are useless for measuring response time, we decided at the outset to discard data from those subjects who made errors on more than 40% of trials.* Thirty subjects from the groups succeeded in making fewer errors than this cut off [italics added] [Rips, 1989, pp. 103–104].

TABLE 2.4
Sample Problems from Experiment 2, with Correct
Response and Relative Number of Inference Steps

	Number of Inference Steps		
	Small		*Large*
Correct			
Response	*Type 1*	*Type 2*	
A = Knight	A: "I am a knave or	A: "I am a knave or	A: "I am a knight
B = Knight	B is a knight."	B is a knight."	or B is a knave."
	B: "I am a knight."	B: "A is a knight."	B: "A is a knight."
A = Knight	A: "I am a knave or	A: "I am a knave or	A: "I am a knight
B = Knight	B is a knight."	B is a knight."	or B is a knave."
	B: "I am a knight."	B: "A is a knight."	B: "A is a knight."
A = Knight	A: "I am a knave or	A: "I am a knave or	A: "I am a knight
B = Knight	B is a knight."	B is a knight."	or B is a knave."
	B: "I am a knight."	B: "A is a knight."	B: "A is a knight."
A = Knight	A: "I am a knave or	A: "I am a knave or	A: "I am a knight
B = Knight	B is a knight."	B is a knight."	or B is a knave."
	B: "I am a knight."	B: "A is a knight."	B: "A is a knight."

Source: Rips, L. J. (1993). The psychology of knights and knaves. *Cognition*, *31*, 85–116. Reprinted with the permission of Elsevier Science Publishers, B.V., and the author.

Results and Discussion

The essential experimental findings are given in the following account:

The critical result is the effect of inference steps: On average, subjects took 25.5 and 23.9 seconds to solve the two types of small-step problems, but 29.5 seconds on the large-step problems. To examine this effect, we performed an analysis of variance of the solution times and then calculated a contrast between the large-step and small-step items. In this analysis, we replaced missing observations due to errors with the mean of the remaining times for the relevant condition. The contrast proved reliable, with . . . p is less than .001. The orthogonal contrast between the two small-step problem types is, however, nonsignificant, . . . p is greater than .10. *This is precisely the pattern we would expect if subjects were solving the problems in the way the model does* [italics added] [Rips, 1989, pp. 104–105].

THE EXPERIMENTS AND THE NATURAL-DEDUCTION MODEL

Rips (1989) defines the following interpretation of the relationship between the experiments and the natural-deduction model.

According to the natural-deduction model, people carry out deduction tasks by constructing mental proofs. They represent the problem information, make further assumptions, draw inferences, and come to conclusions on the basis of this derivation. . . . When subjects thought aloud while solving the puzzles, their statements followed the assume-and-deduce strategy that typifies natural-deduction proofs. Experiment 1 showed that a specific implementation of the model could predict the probability of subjects solving a set of moderately complex and varied puzzles. Experiment 2 generalized this result, demonstrating that response times increased with the number of steps in the underlying proof [italics added] [Rips, 1989, pp. 106–107].

THE EXPERIMENTS AND RIVAL DEDUCTION THEORIES

Rips (1989) compares the natural deduction theory with three other deduction theories.

[We] have interpreted the results only in the natural-deduction framework and have so far neglected other approaches. Since there is, in fact, no consensus about the nature of deductive reasoning (or even whether people are capable of reasoning), we should examine the findings from other points of view. Perhaps some of the alternatives are equally able to account for the findings.

Deduction by Heuristic

Although the present experiments do not directly test rival theories of deductive reasoning, they may still have implications for this debate. Consider, for example, the thesis that people are incapable of deduction outside a narrow range that excludes even simple conditional inferences (Evans, 1982; Pollard, 1982). Although the high error rates that we have . . . discussed lend some support to this view, many of the subjects did reasonably well. [The] most successful subjects scored over 80% in Experiment 1. In Experiment 2, one of our subjects made no errors at all on the 48 critical problems, and 15 additional subjects scored at least 90% correct. Of course, we pre-selected the subjects in the second experiment for accurate responding, so it is hardly surprising to discover that they did well. However, accurate performance on the part of even a few subjects is something that a theory of reasoning must explain. Explaining errors in reasoning is usually easy since . . . there are multiple ways in which they can occur. Correct performance is what taxes a theory, since it suggests more elaborate and more interesting mental processes.

It is possible, certainly, that the successful subjects were right for the wrong reasons — that they based their correct responses on simple heuristics that fell short of true deductive reasoning. But which heuristics? . . . one possibility . . . [One] . . . was a tendency to respond "knave" if the relevant character said I am a knave . . . (or I am not a knight . . .) and to respond "knight" otherwise. However, a glance at [Table 2.4] shows that strict adherence to this heuristic would have produced scores no higher than 25% correct, whereas the obtained rate was 87%. Moreover, this heuristic probably reflects a partial logical insight, since it may well be due to subjects recognizing that neither knights nor knaves can utter the isolated sentence I am a knave. Finally, even if some unknown, non-deductive heuristic could account for the results of the two experiments, it would be hard-pressed to explain protocols such as the one quoted in [Table 2.1]. This subject is in control of the deductive properties of the problem, including implications both of the key terms (i.e., knight, knave, and type) and of the conditionals that she constructs in lines b, f, h, and k. There are no apparent "non-logical" short cuts but, instead, a step-by-step analysis.

Deduction by Pragmatic Schemas

The deficiencies of the heuristic approach also plague more recent theories that tie reasoning to "pragmatic" domains, such as permission-giving (Cheng & Holyoak, 1985; Holland, Holyoak, Nisbett, and Thagard, 1986). A basic problem is that the island of knights and knaves seems as remote from the pragmatic world as it is possible to be. "Pragmatic reasoning," in the intended sense, means that reasoning is a function of schemas that are shaped by everyday circumstance. But a situation in which people always tell the truth or always lie is probably not one that many of us have had experience with. Of course, lying and truth-telling are common enough, and we probably do have schemas for dealing with them. . . . But the mere understanding of lying and truth-telling is insufficient to solve the present problems without further knowledge of the properties of the connectives AND and OR. The results of the experiments strongly suggest that at least the successful subjects do have knowledge of these properties that is independent of any obvious pragmatic domain. The basic evidence for the pragmatic-schemas view comes from experiments showing improved performance in Wason's selection task when the problem is phrased in terms of permissions or restrictions, but not in terms of conditionals that express unfamiliar relations (Cheng & Holyoak, 1985; Griggs & Cox, 1982; Wason & Green, 1984). Although Cheng and Holyoak acknowledge that their "findings need not be interpreted as evidence against the very possibility" of natural deduction, they hold that "people typically reason using schematic knowledge that can be distinguished from . . . context-free syntactic inference rules" (Cheng & Holyoak, 1985, p. 409) and that rules at the level of natural logic "are probably only rarely applied to semantically meaningful material" (Holland et al., 1986, p. 282). However, it is a big step from their results to the latter conclusions. By analogy, it is also true that people don't swim effectively with their feet encased in cement and that their performance improves dramatically when the cement is removed. But it doesn't follow from this that people typically swim by virtue of being freed from cement. To show that "people typically reason using schematic knowledge," one would have to make the case that people use these schemas on most deduction problems, not just that schemas are helpful in the selection task.

Deduction by Mental Models

Finally, consider the proposal by Johnson-Laird (1983) that when people reason deductively they do so by constructing mental models of the content of the problem. On this approach, reasoning begins when a subject sets up an internal diagrammatic model of a situation that is consistent with the given facts of the problem. The subject then surveys the model for a potential conclusion and, if one is found, attempts to find a counterexample to the conclusion by altering the model. If no counterexample appears, the subject adopts the initial conclusion as correct. If there is a counterexample, the first conclusion is rejected and another conclusion examined. This process continues until the subject reaches an acceptable conclusion or decides that no conclusion is valid. Of the alternative theories that we have reviewed, this one comes closest to giving the flavor of the reasoning that the subject of [Table 2.1] engaged in. In this transcript, as well as in the others that we collected, subjects adopt definite hypotheses about the knight-knave status of the character, where these hypotheses may constitute representations for specific states of affairs.

The difficulty with mental models comes in fleshing out the details of the problem-solving process. For example, what would be a mental-models approach to Problem (11) (which we repeat here for reference)?

(11)   We have three inhabitants, A, B, and C, each of whom is a knight or a knave. Two people are said to be of the same type if they are both knights or both knaves. A and B make the following statements:
A: B is a knave.
B: A and C are of the same type.
What is C?

As one possibility, a subject might begin by constructing a mental diagram containing a token for A labeled "knight" to stand for the possibility that A is a knight. Since his statement is true in this model, B must be a knave; so we must add a token for B labeled "knave." This means that B's statement is false, and hence A and C are of different types. We must therefore add a third token for C that also has the "knave" tag. At this point, then, our mental model would look something like this:

(12) knight A
      knave B
      knave C

From this representation, we can read off the tentative conclusion that C is a knave.

We must now ask whether there are other models that are consistent with the given information but in which C is not a knave. To check this, we can attempt to construct a model in which A is labelled "knave." Then B is a knight; so this token must also be changed. Since B's statement is now true, A and C are of the same type; hence token C again gets the "knave" label.

(13) knave A
      knight B
      knave C

But since C is still a knave in this model, our initial conclusion stands. The correct answer is that C is a knave.

How compelling is this account of Problem (1)? Certainly, the "models" in (12) and (13) conform to the possibilities that the subject in [Table 2.1] contemplates; so the theory has some initial plausibility. It's worth recognizing that neither this subject nor any of the other pilot subjects mentioned envisioning or manipulating a situation with tokens corresponding to A, B, and C. But perhaps this can be put down to some difficulty in describing such models. The real trouble is that the theory provides no account of the process that produces and evaluates these models. For example, consider the step that results in adding knight B to the model in (13). The most obvious way to explain this step is to say that we recognized that if A is a knave, his statement is false; that is, it is not the case that B is a knave. We also recognize that if it is not the case that B is a knave, then B is a knight. Johnson-Laird (1983) explicitly denies that this is due to mental inference rules or meaning postulates such as those in [tables 2.2 and 2.3]. He also denies that this kind of reasoning is simply a matter of non-logical heuristics. But assuming this is true, what cognitive mechanism achieves these insights?

Another possibility is that models such as (12) and (13) are put together in a more haphazard way, then checked for consistency with the given information. However, there are two problems with this latter approach. First, it fails to give a good account of systematic protocols such as that in [Table 2.1]. And second, it merely shifts the burden of explanation to the operation of consistency checker. How does the checking process know that (12) is consistent with the problem information without using procedures such as those in [tables 2.2 and 2.3]?

Our suspicion is that whatever plausibility mental models have for these puzzles is due to the fact that they echo the output of the natural-deduction process. . . . The only difference in representation is that the natural-deduction model also includes sentences corresponding to the original statements of the characters and to intermediate inferences. I would claim that the presence of the intermediate sentences is important since the protocol subjects sometimes said things like them. However, the important advantage is that the natural-deduction process explains exactly where all of these items come from. We could, of course, be mistaken in our conjecture of how a mental-models model of these puzzles would go; so we leave it as a challenge to mental modelers: Produce an explicit account of reasoning on knight-knave problems that is (a) theoretically explicit, (b) empirically adequate, and (c) not merely a notational variant of the natural-deduction theory. We don't believe such a challenge can be met and claim that such difficulties are symptomatic of a general failure in the mental-models approach (Macnamara, 1986; Rips, 1986).

There may indeed be alternative theories that can account for the results presented here, but the natural-deduction theory has a headstart. It is consistent with the strategies adopted by the protocol subjects, predicts error rates and solution times in the current experiments, and dovetails with earlier research on other deduction problems [italics added] [Rips, 1989, pp. 107–113].

COMMENTARY

Rips (1989) has provided experimental evidence for his natural-deduction theory and has claimed that rival deduction theories, deduction by heuristics, deduction by pragmatic implications, deduction by mental models, are inadequate in that they cannot account for the details of the logical operations required to solve his difficult knight-knave problems. It must be recognized, however, that theories of reasoning processes must be coherent with the demand characteristics of the experimental task. Knight-knave problems require complicated sequences of logical assumptions and logical derivations and logical tests for contradiction. Heuristic reasoning, by definition, takes shortcuts around these logical sequences; pragmatic reasoning, by definition, subordinates logic operations to practical implications; reasoning by mental models, by definition, relies on imaginal representation of an experimental task and is, therefore, poorly matched to the abstract logical operations required for the knight-knave task.

3

Problem Solving

It is a truism that the pathways of experience lead from being an apprentice to being a master. In recent decades, cognitive psychology and artificial intelligence have attempted to define this transition from novice to expert. Elio and Scharf (1990) developed EUREKA, a computer model of the changes in strategy approach and knowledge organization that take place as the status of novice gives way to the attainment of mastery.

THE GENERAL LOGIC OF EUREKA

The cognitive theory of psychological knowledge schemata provides the general logic for EUREKA.

In the model described below, we propose that interrelated prototypes or schemas emerge with experience. These structures functionally organize related domain-specific expectations, inferences, and methods for solving problems. Furthermore, we assume that the shift in problem-solving strategy is a by-product of the changing content and interassociation of these schemas [Elio and Scharf, 1990, p. 582].

In EUREKA, there is provision for reclassification, modification, and retrieval of strategic knowledge. EUREKA's knowledge can evolve as it experiences and solves physics problems. Knowledge develops in the direction of increasingly abstract categories of physics concepts and principles and sophisticated problem solving methods.

Our model of strategy and knowledge organization shifts is implemented in a system called EUREKA, using a MOPS [Memory Organization Packets]-based representation. The model assumes that some knowledge about physics concepts, equations, and inference rules is initially available in a form that does not specify their usefulness or relevance to any particular type of problem. EUREKA uses this textbook knowledge in conjunction with a means-ends problem-solving strategy to solve force and energy physics problems. After EUREKA solves a problem, the entire problem-solving episode — a set of features, inferences, and solution steps — is stored in a P-MOP [Problem Memory Organization Packet] network that represents long-term memory for previous problem-solving experiences. When a new problem-solving experience is integrated into the P-MOP, it is compared with previous problem-solving knowledge represented on the P-MOPs and indices among P-MOPs. Common portions of the solution method and inferences are abstracted and moved onto newly created P-MOPs organized by new indices. The indices that organize this long-term memory knowledge determine what is retrieved during solution and for generalization. These indices are based on features of the problem. Initially, superficial commonalities and differences of the problems (e.g., inclined plane, pulley) are the types of knowledge abstracted in P-MOPs and used as important discriminating features among P-MOPs. *As EUREKA solves more problems, implicit physics concepts (aspects of the problem not explicitly mentioned in the problem statement), like energies and forces, emerge as the important distinguishing features. These features eventually become the dominant retrieval paths among associated solution methods and domain inferences that have been abstracted as commonalities on P-MOPs. This evolving organization of problem prototype knowledge and the discriminating features organizing it are what underlies the shift in EUREKA's problem-solving strategy and the quality of its solutions* [italics added] [Elio and Scharf, 1990, pp. 584–585].

EUREKA'S INITIAL PHYSICS KNOWLEDGE

EUREKA is initially provided with physics textbook knowledge. The knowledge is neither systematic nor organized in order to simulate the level of comprehension that a novice physics student would have.

The unorganized knowledge is a set of equations and concepts that a novice might know from studying a textbook chapter on force and energy problems. Concepts include real-world objects (e.g., inclined plane, body), relations among objects (e.g., on) and measurable quantities for describing objects and relations between them (e.g., acceleration, friction). This knowledge is unorganized with respect to its potential usefulness to problem solving. For example, we assume that novices could give an equation for Newton's second law even if they could not immediately recognize its applicability to a particular problem [Elio and Scharf, 1990, p. 585].

EUREKA'S PROBLEM SOLVER

The means-ends strategy is used by EUREKA's problem solver to derive a required quantity in a physics problem. If the means-ends strategy fails, EUREKA possesses an interesting meta-strategy that redirects the focus of attention toward a reconstrual of parts of the problem or of their interrelationship.

EUREKA's problem solver is based on a means-end strategy that uses the textbook knowledge and the *P-MOP* knowledge to solve problems. The problem solver also includes an implicit meta-strategy for establishing a focus of attention. This focus of attention directs EUREKA to consider aspects of the problem other than the desired quantity whenever the means-ends approach gets stuck in deriving the problem's desired quantity. These other aspects include relations among objects and features of objects. We call the results of a solution process a problem-solving experience. A problem-solving experience contains retrieved equations, inference rules, derived quantities, inferred concepts, and a kind of "train-of-thought" recording of how the solution method evolved. The entire experience, including any dead ends that were investigated during solution, is then stored in the P-MOP network [Elio and Scharf, 1990, p. 585].

EUREKA'S MEMORY NETWORK

The most interesting feature of the P-MOP network is its dynamic character that reflects changes in the underlying conceptual schemata, as EUREKA develops its strategic knowledge.

The P-MOP network represents EUREKA's long-term memory for past problem-solving experiences as a set of constantly changing problem-type schemas. When given a new problem to solve, EUREKA's problem solver consults the P-MOP network for knowledge that might be relevant to the current problem. Initially, there is no long-term memory knowledge, so the problem solver must rely on the means-ends strategy in conjunction with the textbook knowledge network. Problem-type schemas evolve in the P-MOP network as EUREKA solves each problem and integrates the new problem-solving experience into its existing P-MOP network. After a few problems, the schemas this P-MOP network represents contain few solution methodologies and domain inference rules, primarily organized by surface features the problem had in common. As the P-MOP network accommodates more problem-solving experiences, indices reflecting known concepts and abstract problem features such as "potential energy of the body is known," "the body is moving at time 2," and "there is a normal force acting on the body," emerge as organizing features that lead to more complete solution methodologies and associated domain inference rules. EUREKA's solutions to problems begin to simulate what Larkin et al. (1980) call a knowledge-development approach through the influence of these more expertlike schemas in the P-MOP network [Elio and Scharf, 1990, pp. 585–586].

PROBLEM REPRESENTATION IN EUREKA

The nature of problem representation in EUREKA will be described in this section. For each of two physics problems given to EUREKA, the form of representation and the content of the associated P-MOP will be presented. The first physics problem posed to EUREKA was: "A body of mass 2 slugs is on an inclined plane that has an angle of 30 degrees from the horizontal. The coefficient of friction is 0.3. Find the acceleration of the body" (Elio and Scharf, 1990, p. 586).

For this physics problem, Elio and Scharf (1990) describe its representation and processing in EUREKA in the following account:

EUREKA does not take problems in this natural language form. [Figure 3.1] gives the exact form of Problem 1 given to EUREKA. The problem representation is organized around objects. It also includes the known and desired quantities of the problem. We use the predicate *presence-of* to denote the presence of abstract entities such as forces. The interpretation of *presence-of(body 1, gravity-x-axis)* is "There is a force present that is called gravity-x-axis and it is acting on body 1." We include the forces due to gravity in the initial problem representation. In this problem, the reference frame is specified such that the x-axis is along the inclined plane in the direction of motion and the y-axis is perpendicular to the x-axis.

As EUREKA solves a problem, the problem's representation becomes "enhanced" with inference rules, facts, and solution methodologies. [Figure 3.1] shows the additional knowledge that EUREKA added to Problem 1's representation as it developed a solution. The first type of new knowledge is inference rules that were retrieved from the textbook knowledge network during solution (we explain how this is done later). If the conditions of an inference rule are present as features in a problem, then the representation is augmented with the inference rule and the conclusion of the rule. For example, the inference rules in [Figure 3.1] conclude that normal and frictional forces are

FIGURE 3.1

Problem 1's Initial Representation (a) and Additional
Information Added during the Solution Process (b)

Objects	body1,surface1
Relations	on(body1,surface1)
Features	moving(body1,time2), inclined(surface1), feature (friction (body1,surface1))), mass(body1)
Knowns	(body1,mass), (surface1,incline-angle), gravity, coefficient-friction, (body1, acceleration-y-axis)
Presence-of	(body1,acceleration-x-axis)
Desired	(body1,gravity-x-axis), (body1,gravity-y-axis)

(a)

Presence-of	(body1,friction-x-axis), (body1,normal-y-axis)
Derived	(body1,gravity-x-axis), (body1,sum-of-forces-y-axis) (body1,gravity-y-axis), (body1,normal-y-axis) (body1,friction-x-axis), (body1,sum-of-forces-x-axis) (body1,acceleration-x-axis)
Inference Rules	If a body is on a surface that has friction, Then infer the presence of a frictional force action on the body along x axis
normal	If a body is on something, Then infer the presence of a force acting on the body along the y axis

Soln-Method

(b)

Source: Elio, R. & Scharf, P. (1990). Modeling novice-to-expert shifts in problem solving strategy and knowledge organization. *Cognitive Science*, *14*, 576–639. Reprinted with the permission of the Ablex Publishing Corporation.

acting on the body. We refer to the conclusions of these types of inferences as abstract physics concepts.

The second type of new information in the enhanced representation is derived quantities. These are values of quantities found during the solution process by using equations with known quantities. In this example, seven quantities were derived. The enhanced representation also contains a solution method, drawn in [Figure 3.1a] as a tree structure. The root node of the solution method tree is the desired quantity in the problem. Reading the [Figure 3.1b] solution method tree in a top-down, left-to-right fashion gives the solution process: acceleration along the x-axis, sum of forces along the x-axis, gravity along the x-axis, the relation *on* between the body and the surface, friction along the x-axis, normal force along the y-axis, sum of forces along the y-axis, and gravity along the y-axis. We describe how EUREKA chooses a focus of attention in the section on the problem solver. The solution method also records which equations were used at each step. *It is this enhanced problem representation (i.e., [Figures 3.1a and b] combined) that is subsequently stored in the P-MOP network.*

This enhancement process is an important kind of transformation. The problem that is ultimately stored in the P-MOP network contains many new concepts and quantities inferred during solution [italics added] [Elio and Scharf, 1990, pp. 586–588].

Elio and Scharf (1990) emphasize EUREKA's special inferential ability:

In the case of EUREKA, indexing the enhanced problem representation effectively means that a problem's descriptors are determined by the problem-solving process and not by the problem statement's original form. For example, an inference that there is a force acting along the x-axis introduces a new, additional descriptor for some problem situation. *Thus, EUREKA is not limited to describing and learning problem schemas in terms of the descriptors found in the problem statement, but rather will learn schemas based on inferred concepts using its textbook and existing P-MOP knowledge* [italics added] [Elio and Scharf, 1990, p. 588].

THE P-MOP IN EUREKA

The P-MOP is a crucial component of the EUREKA system. Elio and Scharf (1990) summarize its major characteristics in the following account:

Two types of knowledge are organized in the P-MOP network: Specific problem-solving experiences, a term we use interchangably [*sic*] with enhanced problem representations (see [Figure 3.1]), and P-MOPs, which represent a collection of common features (domain inference rules, solution methods, and problem features). When we say that a P-MOP "organizes" other P-MOPs and specific experiences, we mean that (a) the P-MOP contains information common to a number of other P-MOPs and specific experiences and (b) these other structures are accessible from this P-MOP via indices or retrieval paths that represent their differences from each other.

The root node of the P-MOP network is a P-MOP that defines a "generic physics problem." This is shown as P-MOP1 in [Figure 3.2]. Following Kolodner's (1983b) terminology, a P-MOP has a set of *norms* that represent commonalities of the knowledge it organizes. The norms on P-MOP1 are a collection of predicates for specifying how physics problems can be described, namely in terms of things that are known and desired, objects, features of objects, and relations among objects.

Problem-solving experiences are organized according to their differences from the norms appearing on a P-MOP. As the root node of the network, P-MOP1 organizes incoming problem-solving experiences according to how they differ from its norms, that is, differences in knowns, objects, object relations, and so forth. Each difference from a norm is called an *index*. An index is a predicate-value pair, such as *desired(acceleration, body1)*, that points to the representation of a specific problem-solving experience or to another P-MOP. A predicate must appear as a norm before it can serve as an index. As we explain below, any predicate that appears in an enhanced problem representation, in addition to the ones initially defining P-MOP1, can become norms on a P-MOP. Once a predicate is recognized as a potential commonality and becomes a norm on a particular P-MOP, it is also eligible to become an index to organize similar problem-solving knowledge from that P-MOP.

Each time EUREKA finishes a problem, it stores the final enhanced problem representation into the P-MOP network. [Figure 3.2] shows what the network would look like after Problems 1 and 2 have been solved and their enhanced representations integrated into the P-MOP network. The English version of Problem 2 is:

A body of mass 3 slugs is on a frictionless inclined plane that has an angle of 40 degrees from the horizontal. Find the acceleration of the body.

The enhanced representations of the two problems are indexed from P-MOP1 according to their differences from P-MOP1's norms. For example, Problem 1's representation and Problem 2's representation differ from P-MOP1's *feature* norm, which only says that objects have features, but not what those features actually are. To minimize the complexity of the figure, different indices pointing to the same knowledge structure are shown beside a single line. Thus, there are two different indices from P-MOP1 to Problem 1's enhanced representation.

FIGURE 3.2

The P-MOP Representation of Problems 1 and 2

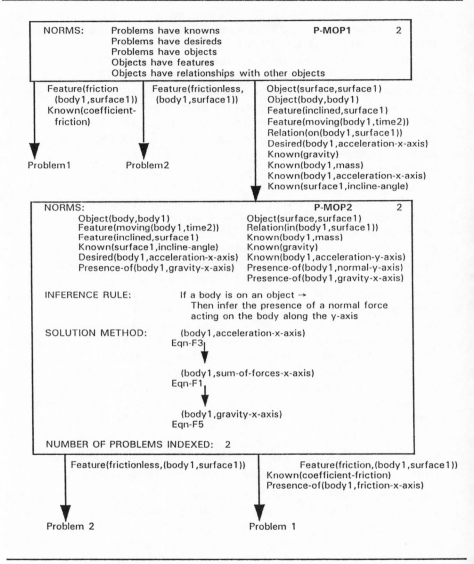

Source: Elio, R. & Scharf, P. (1990). Modeling novice-to-expert shifts in problem solving strategy and knowledge organization. *Cognitive Science*, *14*, 576–639. Reprinted with the permission of the Ablex Publishing Corporation.

P-MOP2 in [Figure 3.2] represents the commonalities and discriminating features of the two problem-solving experiences. Both problems involve a moving body on an inclined surface, a gravity force, a normal force acting on the body, several known quantities, and the acceleration of the body along the plane as the desired quantity. These are the norms of P-MOP1. Because the inference rule, *If a body is on an object, then there is a normal force acting on the body along the y-axis*, is used in the solution of both problems, it is also stored on P-MOP2. In addition to containing commonalities between these two problems, P-MOP2 also keeps track of the differences for indexing these problems. In this example, features regarding friction are the differences. Problem 2 is indexed from P-MOP2 by the feature that the surface is frictionless. Problem 1 is indexed in three ways from P-MOP2. Indices serve as directed retrieval paths for accessing knowledge structures from each other in the network. The information in one knowledge structure is reached from another by meeting the specifications of the index connecting them.

The P-MOP restructuring mechanisms, which are discussed in greater detail below, also compare the solution methods of the two problems and store common solution steps on the P-MOP. In this case, only part of the solution method was common between the two problems. The solution method shown on P-MOP2 is the entire solution method EUREKA developed for Problem 2. Because friction was not common between the two problems, the portion of Problem 1's solution that dealt with friction does not appear on P-MOP2 but instead remains on Problem 1's enhanced representation [Elio and Scharf, 1990, pp. 588–591].

THE TEXTBOOK NETWORK IN EUREKA

EUREKA's textbook network is presented in detail in Appendix A. In this section, an overview will be given of three types of knowledge found in the network: concepts, inference rule, and equation.

Concepts in the textbook network include physical objects, features of objects, and relationships between objects. *Body* is an example of a physical object with *mass* as a feature; it may have the relation *on* with another object that is a surface. Forces, like gravitational, frictional, and normal force, and energies, such as potential and kinetic energy, are also concepts in the textbook network.

Inference rules are implications of the form P $\rightarrow$ Q, where P is a set of conditions that must be present in the problem representation in order to add Q to the problem representation. For example, the two conditions necessary for inferring friction using Inf-A in Appendix A are that a body must be a surface and that there is friction between the body and the surface.

The third type of knowledge contained in the textbook are equations describing kinematic, force, and energy relationships. The equations contain a left-hand side, a right-hand side, and possibly one or more constraints. For example, the constrain of Eqn-E14 in Appendix A requires that the object of interest be on a surface. Constraints of an equation must appear in the problem representation for the equation to be used [Elio and Scharf, 1990, pp. 591–592].

The nature of the interrelationships among concepts, inference rules, and equations is summarized in the following account:

Concepts are associated with each other through simple a-kind-of relations and with the inference rules and equations in which they participate. A concept is associated with an inference rule if the concept appears in the condition side of the inference. A concept is associated with an equation if it appears anywhere in the equation. Besides these associational relations, we have no further assumptions about the representations of this type of textbook knowledge [Elio and Scharf, 1990, p. 592].

THE FOCUS OF ATTENTION IN EUREKA

To solve a physics problem, EUREKA must derive a desired quantity. The focus of attention mechanism constitutes EUREKA's control on its set of cognitive maneuvers between and within concepts, inferences, and equations. The cognitive control exercised by the focus of attention is one of the more interesting features of the EUREKA system. Following a general description, the detailed operations of the focus of attention will be illustrated by reference to the first physics problem discussed earlier in this section.

The focus of attention is important because it derives the retrieval of inferences and equations from the textbook knowledge network and their incorporation into the evolving problem representation. For each focus of attention, EUREKA retrieves all associated inference rules and relevant equations. If the conditions of an inference rule are satisfied by features of the problem representation, both the rule and its conclusion are added to the problem representation. Typically, if EUREKA wishes to use an equation to solve for some quantity and that equation contains other unknown quantities, then one of those unknown quantities becomes the new focus of attention. Thus, the focus of attention also drives the creation of goal-subgoal trees that record the relations between each focus of attention and the associated equations EUREKA has retrieved. These goal-subgoal structures represent the evolving solution method and are also added to the problem representation. If EUREKA uses all of its equations for its focus of attention and has not solved the problem, it selects a new focus of attention from other features in the problem representation, some of which may have resulted from inferences. These features in turn might enable EUREKA to continue its equation-retrieval process. A problem is solved when its desired quantity has been derived [Elio and Scharf, 1990, p. 593].

Elio and Scharf (1990) present the following account of the focus of attention mechanism as applied to the first physics problem:

EUREKA's first step in solving Problem 1 is to set its focus of attention to be the desired quantity, which is acceleration of the body along the x-axis. This creates a goal that is added to the problem representation. EUREKA next retrieves all inferences from the textbook knowledge network that are associated with the current focus of attention. In this case, there are none associated with acceleration. EUREKA then retrieves from the textbook network all equations that have the focus of attention as a variable. In order to be used, equations must have their constraints satisfied and must not contain more than one unknown variable other than the focus of attention. This leaves only Eqn-F3; sum-of-forces-x-axis = mass * acceleration-x-axis.

Having retrieved this equation, EUREKA works on deriving the remaining unknowns so the equation can be solved for acceleration. The mass of the body appears as a known quantity in the problem representation, so the next focus of attention is sum-of-forces-x-axis. At this stage of the problem, the goal-subgoal structure in the solution method indicates that (a) the first focus of attention was acceleration-along-x-axis, (b) Eqn-F3 was retrieved and selected to solve for this quantity, and (c) the next focus of attention was sum-of-forces-x-axis [Figure 3.1b].

The focus of attention is now sum-of-forces-x-axis. EUREKA finds no inferences associated with this concept but does retrieve four equations from the textbook knowledge network. Only equation Eqn-F1 (see Appendix B) has all its constraints satisfied and does not contain more than one unknown. As mentioned previously, this equation's right-hand side is constructed by a procedure that sums all of the forces along the x-axis. Gravity along the x-axis is the only force contained in the current problem representation. Therefore, the Eqn-F1 is instantiated as sum-of-forces-x-axis = gravity-x-axis and the next focus of attention is gravity-x-axis.

Gravity is not associated with any inferences but does appear in equation Eqn-F5. At this point in the growing problem representation, all variables in this equation appear as known quantities. As a result, gravity-x-axis is marked as derived and added to the problem representation. This goal is popped, EUREKA goes back to Eqn-F1, and the focus of attention reverts to sum-of-forces-x-axis (see [Figure 3.1]). Recall that Eqn-F1 is a vector summation of forces along the x-axis, without specifying what these forces are. The only force EUREKA knows about at this point is gravity along the x-axis. It formulates the equation using this as the only force and asks the teacher if all the relevant forces have been identified. The force due to friction is missing, so the teacher responds "no" and EUREKA knows it cannot solve this equation correctly at this time. Note that the teacher does not specify what is missing. Over time, EUREKA learns what the relevant forces are for this type of problem, so when it asks about these equations after some experience, the teacher will respond "yes [you have all the relevant forces there]." Getting back to the example, there are no other equations associated with the current focus of attention, sum-of-forces-x-axis. Therefore, EUREKA changes its focus of attention back to the parent goal, acceleration-along-x-axis. However, there are no other eligible equations for deriving acceleration.

Once EUREKA has arrived back at its top goal, the desired quantity, with no answer and no more equations to use, it must find a new focus of attention. There are a number of other aspects about the problem that could serve as focuses of attention and possibly get the solution moving again. Specifically, there are four leads EUREKA considers in this order: recently inferred concepts that were not in the original problem representation, relations among objects in the problem, features of objects in the problem, and the objects themselves. This approach to finding a new focus of attention constitutes an implicit meta-strategy and serves to keep EUREKA on its current tangent, even though it has run out of equations. Intuitively, it seems reasonable that the most recent changes to the representation should influence the solution method, but we have no data on whether a meta-strategy favoring recently inferred concepts is a correct characterization of novice problem-solving behavior.

At this point in Problem 1's enhanced representation, there are no newly inferred concepts. The next lead to follow is relations, so EUREKA arbitrarily selects the relation *on* and retrieves five associated inference rules. Two of these five inference rules have their conditions met in the current representation:

Inf-A If   a body is on a surface and there is a friction between the body and
              the surface
      Then there is the presence-of-friction force acting on the body along the
              x-axis
Inf-B If   a body is on an object
      Then there is the presence-of a normal force acting on the body along
              the y-axis

The problem representation is augmented with the conclusions of these rules. EUREKA then goes to the textbook knowledge network to retrieve equations but the concept *on* has no associated equations. Because this is a dead end, another focus of attention is needed. The problem representation now has newly inferred concepts, so EUREKA arbitrarily makes one of them, friction-x-axis, the new focus of attention and proceeds to retrieve associated inferences and equations.

EUREKA continues in this manner until the original desired quantity is derived and the problem is solved. This yields the solution tree shown in

[Figure 3.1]. At this point, the enhanced problem representation, including the solution tree in [Figure 3.1], is stored in the P-MOP network [Elio and Scharf, 1990, pp. 594–596].

EUREKA'S NOVICE AND EXPERT PROTOCOLS

Elio and Scharf (1990) offer the following protocols for understanding what EUREKA might be doing differentially when it solves problems as a novice and as an expert:

Although we did not program EUREKA to simulate a verbal protocol during problem solving, it is easy to depict such a protocol using the structures in [Figures 3.3a and 3.3b] and Problem 1 as an example. As a novice solving Problem 1, EUREKA has no prior knowledge in the P-MOP network, so its solution is based strictly on means-ends analysis. The protocol it could give as it constructed the solution method in [Figure 3.1] might go as follows:

EUREKA: I need an equation to solve for acceleration. Eqn-F3 is a possibility. Sum-of-forces is an unknown in Eqn-F3.

I need an equation to solve for sum-of-forces. Eqn-F1 is a possibility.

Gravity is an unknown in Eqn-F1. I need an equation to solve for gravity.

Eqn-F5 is the best possibility. I know all the other quantities in Eqn-F5, so I can solve for gravity.

I substitute gravity into Eqn-F1 and believe that I know all the forces needed to solve for sum-of-forces. Is this correct?

Teacher: No, you haven't identified all the forces.

EUREKA: So I can't solve Eqn-F1 and I have no other ways to get acceleration right now.

I notice that the body is ON something. If a body is on something, then there is a frictional force acting on that body. I could try solving for friction. The equations I know for doing that are. . . .

and so on.

In order to generate a protocol for this same problem after the problem-solving knowledge in [Figures 3.3a and 3.3b] developed, EUREKA could mention constraints that are matched (indices traversed), deep features that are inferred (inference rules on P-MOPs), and possible solution methods (also found on P-MOPs). For Problem 1, P-MOP1 does not provide any useful information. P-MOP10 can be reached via a number of inclined-plane indices, so the expert solution protocol to Problem 1 might begin with any one of them as the first constraint satisfied:

FIGURE 3.3a
The P-MOP Network after All Ten Problems Are Solved

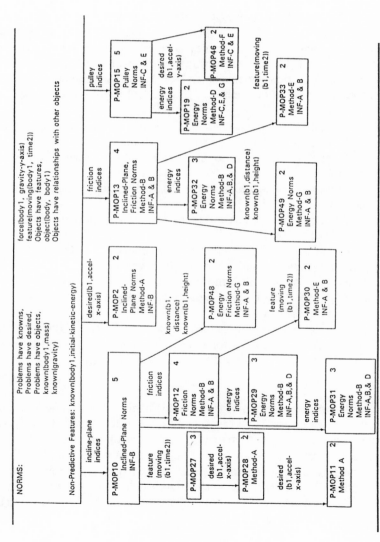

FIGURE 3.3b

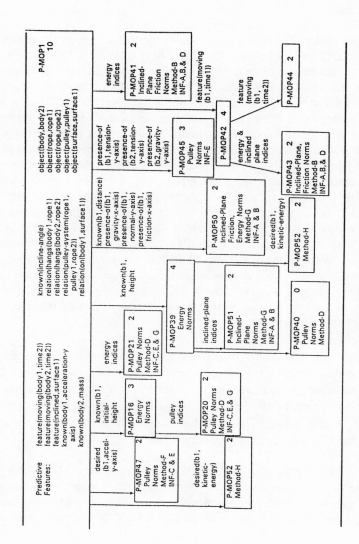

Source: Elio, R. & Scharf, P. (1990). Modeling novice-to-expert shifts in problem solving strategy and knowledge organization. *Cognitive Science, 14,* 576–639. Reprinted with the permission of the Ablex Publishing Corporation.

EUREKA: There is an on-relationship between the body and the surface [*one possible path to P-MOP10*]. There is a normal force acting on the body [*inference rule on P-MOP10*].

The coefficient of friction is known [*one of several indices to P-MOP12 which is preferred because it indexes the most experiences*].

I know there is a normal force and a frictional force acting on the body [*inference rules on P-MOP12*] and I know how to solve for normal force acting on this body [*Method B on P-MOP12*].

The body is also in motion along a surface [*moving to P-MOP30*], which means that the frictional force can be found by [*Method E on P-MOP30*].

At this point, P-MOP30 indexes two problems, one of which is Problem 1. Having reached Problem 1's representation (see [Figure 3.1]), EUREKA would only need the leftmost subtree because it has already figured out that there are normal and frictional forces acting on the body and what methods would be appropriate for deriving them. Even if the solution to Problem 1 were completely forgotten, EUREKA would have generated a nearly complete solution in this forward-working manner. We think it is important that the qualitative shift in solution methods comes not from retrieving past solution trees, but from remembering and recalling relevant inferences about the problem scenarios which trigger principles, which in turn have associated contexts that specify conditions of applicability and further tests. P-MOPs 1, 10, 12, and 30 used in this hypothetical protocol comprise what we consider to be a complete configuration of constraints. The norms found on the P-MOPs, particularly those that are also predictive features, can also be viewed as expectations for the type of problem EUREKA is currently working on. *The hypothetical protocols for Problem 1 illustrate how a shift to a knowledge-development strategy is supported by the kind of knowledge abstracted in the P-MOP network and the manner in which it is organized and restructured with experience* [italics added] [Elio and Scharf, 1990, pp. 619–620].

Elio and Scharf (1990) point out that as a result of EUREKA's experience with additional problems beyond that of Problems 1 and 2, its strategic knowledge organization increases in sophistication, as shown in the complex networks of Figures 3.3a and 3.3b compared with those of Figures 3.1a and 3.1b; EUREKA has moved from novice knowledge organization to expert knowledge organization.

The problem-solving trace and protocols demonstrated how EUREKA's final knowledge organization evolves from a novice-like organization based on surface features to an expertlike organization characterized by known quantities and abstract physics entities. In its novice stages, EUREKA has no option but to use means-ends analysis to solve problems. When a few problem-solving experiences are indexed, the initial P-MOP network is organized around surface features. As more problems are solved, known quantities and inferred physics entities become the discriminating and characteristic features upon which organizational structure is based. *EUREKA begins to prefer indices about known quantities and abstract physics entities like forces because, over time, they emerge as the best discriminating features of problem-solving knowledge* [italics added] [Elio and Scharf, 1990, p. 621].

COMMENTARY

Elio and Scharf (1990) have demonstrated how, in EUREKA, knowledge concerning the domain of elementary physics problems is acquired, organized, reorganized, and abstracted with consequent augmentation of the system's power. Unlike expert systems in general, which are only performance motivated, EUREKA provides a detailed developmental account of its transitional progress as it achieves the status of an expert problem solver. Important advances in the understanding of how human novices become human experts could be achieved by a comparison of EUREKA, serving as a computational model, with research protocols produced by human subjects.

4

Analogical Thinking

THE NATURE OF ANALOGICAL THINKING

Thinking is sometimes deductive, sometimes inductive, and sometimes analogical. Deductive thinking has the character of formal logical representations and derivations; inductive thinking looks to the accumulated balance of positive and negative instances; analogical thinking seeks correspondences between the features of two sets of concepts or objects. Analogical thought can serve the purpose of setting forth an explanation by the correspondence of elements in known situations with those in fully understood situations. Scientific discovery processes are often aided by analogical thought. In political, economic, and intellectual movements, analogies are widely used in argumentation and persuasion. Analogies in the form of expressive metaphors and similes are prevalent in classical literature and everyday language.

A theory of analogical thinking and a computational model of the theory has been developed by Holyoak and Thagard (1989). Their interesting research will be described, and the implications of their theory and model will be discussed in a commentary section.

THE GENERAL LOGIC OF ANALOGICAL MAPPING BY CONSTRAINT SATISFACTION

The general logic of analogical mapping requires a set of criteria or constraints that delimit the essential correspondences or similitudes between two analogs, typically a source analog and a target analog. Three delimiting and interacting constraints are stipulated in the theory advanced by Holyoak and Thagard (1989, p. 295):

The structural constraint of isomorphism encourages mappings that maximize the consistency of relational correspondences between the elements of the two analogs. *The constraint of semantic similarity* supports mapping hypotheses to the degree that mapped predicates have similar meanings. *The constraint of pragmatic centrality* favors mappings involving elements the analogist believes to be important in order to achieve the purpose for which the analogy is being used [italics added].

THE ANALOGICAL CONSTRAINT MAPPING ENGINE MODEL OF ANALOGICAL MAPPING

Holyoak and Thagard (1989) developed Analogical Constraint Mapping Engine (ACME), a cooperative algorithm for analogical mapping that is directed toward the satisfaction of the sets of interactive constraints described in the previous section. The rationale for the use of a cooperative algorithm in analogical mapping is set forth in the following assertions.

Several properties of an information-processing task can provide cues that a cooperative algorithm may be appropriate. A cooperative algorithm for parallel constraint satisfaction is preferable to any serial decision procedure when: (a) a global decision is composed of a number of constituent decisions, (b) each constituent decision should be based upon multiple constraints, (c) the outcome of the global decision could vary depending upon the order in which constraints are applied and constituent decisions are made, and (d) there is no principled justification for preferring any particular order of constraints or of constituent decisions. Analogical mapping using constraints exhibits all of these features [Holyoak and Thagard, 1989, p. 306].

ACME, as a parallel architecture, constructs a network of nodes or units that represent hypotheses and produces an optimal mapping as an outcome of program processing. There are a number of general features in the design of ACME's network, its nodes, and hypotheses bearing out the relationship between the source analog and the target analog.

Each possible hypothesis about a possible pairing of an element from the source with a corresponding element of the target is assigned to a node or *unit*. Each unit has an *activation level*, ranging between some minimum and maximum values, which indicates the plausibility of the corresponding hypothesis, with higher activation indicating greater plausibility. Inferential dependencies between mapping hypotheses are represented by *weights* or *links* between units. Supporting evidence is given a negative weight. . . . The input to the program consists of predicate-calculus representations of the source and target analogs, plus optional information about semantic similarity and pragmatic importance. It is assumed that a mapping may be computed either from a target analog to a source or vice versa. It is conjectured that the direction of the mapping will vary depending upon the use of the analogy and the knowledge of the analogist. If the source is much more familiar than the target, then it may be best to try to map source elements to target elements. On the other hand, if the source is much more complicated than the target or if the target contains highly salient elements, then the analogist may attempt to map from the target to the source. . . . When given two structures as input, ACME automatically generates a network in accord with the constraints postulated by the theory. . . . As units are established, links are formed between them to implement the constraint of structural consistency. All links are symmetrical, with the same weight regardless of direction. . . . In addition to the units representing mapping hypotheses, the network includes two special units. The *semantic unit* is used to convey information about the system's prior assessment of the degree of semantic similarity between each pair of meaningful concepts in the target and source, and the *pragmatic unit* similarly is used to convey information about the pragmatic importance of possible correspondences. The semantic-similarity constraint is enforced by placing excitatory links from the semantic unit to all units representing mappings between predicates. The weights on these links are made proportional to the degree of semantic similarity between the mapped concepts. Similarly, the pragmatic-centrality constraint is represented by weights on links connecting the pragmatic unit to relevant mapping units [Holyoak and Thagard, 1989, pp. 308–312].

GENERAL APPLICATIONS OF ACME

As the implementation of a general theory of analogical thinking, ACME should be able to apply its analogical mapping functions to analogical problem-solving, analogical argumentation, analogical explanation, and analogical metaphor.

Major contexts for analogy use include problem solving, when the solution to one problem suggests a solution to a similar one; argumentation, when similarities between two situations are used to contend that what is true in one situation is likely to be true in the other; and explanation, when a familiar topic is used to provide understanding of a less familiar one. In addition, analogical reasoning is also used to understand formal analogies of the sort found in mathematics, as well as metaphors, which can be employed to serve both explanatory and more aesthetic functions [Holyoak and Thagard, 1989, p. 318].

It is impressive that ACME does, in fact, apply its mapping algorithms to the many various contexts in which analogical reasoning takes place. Table 4.1 summarizes the types of analogies mapped by ACME and some network characteristics of each mapping.

TABLE 4.1
Summary of Applications of ACME

Analogs	Number of Units	Number of Symmetric Links
Lightbulb/radiation problems (four versions) (Holyoak & Koh, 1987)	169–192	1,373–1,773
Fortress/radiation problems (Gick & Holyoak, 1980)	41	144
Cannibals and missionaries/farmer's dilemma problems (Gholson et al., 1986)	144	973
Contras interference	95	169
Politics interference (two versions)	55–67	308–381
Water-flow/heat-flow explanation (two versions) (Falkenhainer et al., 1986)	62–127	317–1,010
Solar system/atom explanation (Falkenhainer et al., 1986)	93	733
Jealous animal stories (six versions) (Gentner & Toupin, 1986)	125–214	1,048–1,873
Addition/union	162	1,468
Attribute mapping	43	220
Midwife/Socrates (three versions) (Kittay, 1987)		
Chemical analogies (eight different analogies) (Thagard et al., 1989)		

Source: Holyoak, K. J. and Thagard, P. (1989). Analogical mapping by constraint satisfaction. *Cognitive Science, 13*, 295–355. Reprinted with the permission of the Ablex Publishing Corporation.

ACME's analogical reasoning ability can be appreciated by considering two extremes in its range of applications. These are ACME's ability to process formal mathematical analogies on the one hand and literary metaphors on the other hand.

APPLICATION OF ACME TO A FORMAL MATHEMATICAL ANALOGY

ACME was posed the problem of discovering a formal analogy between two mathematical concepts: the addition of numbers and the union of sets. The analogy is formal in that it depends only on isomorphic or structural constraints and is devoid of semantic and pragmatic content.

[Table 4.2] presents a formal analogy between addition of numbers and union of sets. . . . Both addition and union have the abstract mathematical properties of commutativity, associativity, and the existence of an identity element (0 for numbers and φ for sets). ACME was given predicate-calculus representations of these two analogs, with no identical elements (note that number equality and set equality are given distinct symbols), and with all semantic weights set equal to the minimal value. This analogy is quite complex, as many propositions have the same predicates (sum or union), and many symbols representing intermediate results must be sorted out. Note that the representations given to the program did not explicitly group the components of each analog into three distinct equations. In the absence of any semantic or pragmatic information, only weights based upon isomorphism, coupled with the type restriction, provided information about the optimal mapping.

As the output in [Table 4.3] indicates, ACME settles to a complete solution to this formal mapping problem after 59 cycles. The model is thus able to derive a unique mapping in the absence of any overlap between the elements of the source and target. ACME's ability to deal with such examples is crucially dependent upon its parallel constraint-satisfaction algorithm [Holyoak and Thagard, 1989, pp. 340–341].

TABLE 4.2

Formal Isomorphism between Addition of Numbers and Union of Sets

Property	Addition	Union
Commutativity	$N1 + N2 = N2 + N1$	$S1 \cup S2 = S2 \cup S1$
Associativity	$N3 + (N4 + N5) =$	$S3 \cup [S4 \cup S5] =$
	$(N3 + N4) + N5$	$[S3 \cup S4] \cup S5$
Identity	$N6 + 0 = N6$	$S6 \cup \varnothing = S6$

Predicate-Calculus Representations

Numbers	(sum (num1 num2 num10) n1)
	(sum (num2 num1 num11) n2)
	(num_eq (num10 num11) n3)
	(sum (num5 num6 num12) n3)
	(sum (num4 num12 num13) n5)
	(sum (num4 num5 num14) n6)
	(sum (num14 num6 num15) n7)
	(num_eq (num13 num15) n8)
	(sum (num20 zero num20) n9)
Sets	(union (set1 set2 set10) s1)
	(union (set2 set1 set11) s2)
	(set_eq (set10 set11) s3)
	(union (set5 set6 set12) s4)
	(union (set4 set12 set13) s5)
	(union (set4 set5 set14) s6)
	(union (set14 set6 set15) s7)
	(set_eq (set13 set15) s8)
	(union (set20 empty-set set20) s9)

Source: Holyoak, K. J. and Thagard, P. (1989). Analogical mapping by constraint satisfaction. *Cognitive Science*, *13*, 295–355. Reprinted with the permission of the Ablex Publishing Corporation.

TABLE 4.3

Output after Running Addition/Union Analogy

Network has settled by cycle 59.
Test: TEST0 Total Times: 60
Mon May 2 10:40:03 EDT 1988
Analogy between numbers and sets.
Units not yet reached asymptote: 0
Goodness of network: 3.31
Calculating the best mappings after 60 cycles.
Best mapping of NUM10 is SET 10. 0.79
Best mapping of NUM2 is SET 2. 0.82
Best mapping of NUM1 is SET 1. 0.82
Best mapping of NUM11 is SET 11. 0.79
Best mapping of NUM12 is SET 12. 0.82
Best mapping of NUM6 is SET 6. 0.82
Best mapping of NUM5 is SET 5. 0.82
Best mapping of NUM13 is SET 13. 0.79
Best mapping of NUM4 is SET 4. 0.82
Best mapping of NUM14 is SET 14. 0.82
Best mapping of NUM15 is SET 15. 0.79
Best mapping of NUM20 is SET 20. 0.66
Best mapping of ZERO is EMPTY-SET. 0.66
Best mapping of NUM_EQ is SET_EQ. 0.57
Best mapping of SUM is UNION. 0.83

Source: Holyoak, K. J. and Thagard, P. (1989). Analogical mapping by constraint satisfaction. *Cognitive Science*, *13*, 295–355. Reprinted with the permission of the Ablex Publishing Corporation.

APPLICATION OF ACME TO A LITERARY METAPHOR

ACME's ability to map metaphors was tested by confronting it with two versions of a classical metaphor in which Socrates is the midwife of an idea. The correct version is the straightforward metaphor, but in the incorrect version, misleading and confusing information is introduced. In the following account, the correct version is referred to as the isomorphic version.

The run reported in the first column [of Table 4.4] used the isomorphic version without any pragmatic weights. The network settles with a correct set of mappings after 34 cycles. Thus Socrates maps to the midwife, his student to the mother, the student's intellectual partner to the father, and the idea to the child. (Note that there is a homomorphic mapping of the predicates thinks_about and

TABLE 4.4

Best Mappings, with Asymptotic Activation Levels, for Objects and Predicates in Three Versions of the Socrates/Midwife Metaphor

	Versions					
	Isomorphic Nonpragmatic		Nonisomorphic Nonpragmatic		Nonisomorphic Pragmatic	
Cycles to Settle	34		105		83	
Objects						
Socrates	obj_midwife	.87	obj_father	.80	obj_midwife	.86
obj_student	obj_mother	.69	obj_mother	.69	obj_mother	.69
obj_partner	obj_father	.81	none		obj_father	.80
obj_idea	obj_child	.90	obj_child	.69	obj_child	.70
*obj_soc-midwife	—		obj_midwife	.84	none	
*obj_soc-wife	—		obj_mother	.69	obj_mother	.69
*obj_soc-child	—		obj_child	.69	obj_child	.65
*obj_hemlock	—		none		none	
Predicates						
philosopher	midwife	.58	none		midwife	.81
student	mother	.59	none		none	
intellectual_partner	father	.57	none		father	.57
idea	child	.59	none		child	.58
introduces	matches	.77	none		matches	.67
formulates	conceives	.72	conceives	.27	conceives	.31
thinks_about	in_labor_with	.36	none		none	
tests_truth	in_labor_with	.36	none		none	
knows_truth_or_falsify	gives_birth_to	.72	gives_birth_to	.72	gives_birth_to	.72
helps	helps	.77	helps	.79	helps	.80
cause	cause	.84	cause	.84	cause	.84
*poison	—		none		none	
*drink	—		none		none	
*Father	—		father	.70	none	
*midwife	—		midwife	.70	none	
*mother	—		mother	.69	mother	.69
*child	—		child	.69	none	
*matches	—		matches	.78	none	
*conceives	—		conceives	.48	conceives	.43
*in_labor_with	—		in_labor_with	.74	in_labor_with	.74
*gives_birth_to	—		gives_birth_to	.46	gives_birth_to	.43

*Elements with an asterisk appeared only in nonisomorphic version. Elements that map to "none" have no mapping unit with activation greater than 20.

Source: Holyoak, K. J. and Thagard, P. (1989). Analogical mapping by constraint satisfaction. *Cognitive Science*, *13*, 295–355. Reprinted with the permission of the Ablex Publishing Corporation.

tests_truth to in_labor_with.) The propositions expressing causal relations in the two analogs are not essential here; deletion of them still allows a complete mapping to be discovered [Holyoak and Thagard, 1989, p. 344].

In the nonisomorphic version or incorrect version, ACME's performance in mapping the metaphor is potentially degraded by the introduction of inappropriate data.

The nonisomorphic version contains the information that Socrates drinks hemlock juice, which is of course irrelevant to the metaphor. Far worse, the representation encodes the information that Socrates himself was matched to his wife by a midwife; and that Socrates' wife had a child with the help of this midwife. Clearly, this nonisomorphic extension will cause the structural and semantic constraints on mapping to support a much more superficial set of correspondences between the two situations. And indeed, in this second run, ACME finds only the barest fragments of the intended metaphoric mappings when the network settles after 105 cycles. Socrates' midwife now maps to the midwife in the source, and Socrates' wife and child map to the source mother and child. Socrates himself simply maps to the father. Most of the other crucial objects and predicates (other than cause and helps, which map to themselves) have no good mappings. The only major pieces of the intended analogy that survive are the mappings between the student and the mother and between the idea and the child.

Note, however, that the original statement of the metaphor, "Socrates is a midwife of ideas," provides some direct pragmatic guidance as to the intended mappings. Clearly, Socrates must map to the midwife, and the idea must map to something. This is precisely the kind of knowledge that ACME can represent using pragmatic weights. Accordingly, in a further run the mappings between propositions sl and ml and between the elements of those propositions (i.e., sl = ml, Socrates = obj_midwife, and philosopher = midwife) were marked as PRESUMED; and proposition s4 and its elements (i.e., s4, obj_idea, and idea) were marked as IMPORTANT. The right column of [Table 4.1] reports the results for the nonisomorphic version of the metaphor after these pragmatic weights are introduced. The pragmatic information was sufficient to allow almost complete recovery of the abstract metaphoric mappings. The network settled after 83 cycles. Socrates again maps to the midwife, and the partner to the father; almost all of the appropriate predicate mappings, such as those between idea and child and between introduces and conceives, are also recovered. Note that some of the more superficial mappings of objects, such as between Socrates' wife and the mother, also emerge. *The behavior of the program across these versions of the metaphor thus dramatically illustrates both the power and the limitations of purely structural constraints, and the crucial role of pragmatic knowledge in finding abstract mappings in the face of misleading information* [italics added] [Holyoak and Thagard, 1989, pp. 344–347].

COMMENTARY

ACME's mapping performance is algorithmic, and, therefore, it is not surprising that it should fall short of the flexibility and power found in human analogical reasoning. For example, ACME cannot handle the significant reasoning operation of propositional converses. Thus, ACME is unable to map the converse relation between the inscribed proposition and the circumscribed proposition in plane and solid geometry.

ACME, as a computational approach to the generation and comprehension of analogies and metaphors, needs to be provided with vast amounts of knowledge that would enable it to be useful in complex human exposition of concepts, facts, and allusions. This knowledge requirement can be clearly seen in the following account of metaphor and theories of psychotherapy:

A metaphoric analysis of psychotherapy . . . contributes an understanding that is immediate, holistic, and idiographic. Psychoanalysis has a literary, classical, and dramatic metaphor (e.g., the incestuous conflicts of Oedipus, the obsessional struggles of Hamlet). Behavior therapy has a physiological, physicalistic, and mechanistic metaphor (e.g., deconditioning of anxiety responses, systematic training in adaptive behavior). Client-centered therapy has a personalistic, individualistic, and ideational metaphor (e.g., a search for self-identity, the discovery of personal values). Cognitive therapy has a rationalistic, logical, and educative metaphor (e.g., multiple and flexible rather than single and rigid interpretations of the meaning of life events, quality of cognition as precursor to quality of feeling). . . . These metaphors have the advantage of quickly capturing distinctive qualities in systems of psychotherapy [Wagman, 1988, p. 12].

5

Scientific Discovery

SCIENTIFIC DISCOVERY AND ARTIFICIAL INTELLIGENCE

The General Logic of BACON.3

The process of scientific discovery depends on the detection of patterns in data and the summary representation of these patterns in theoretical terms. BACON.3 uses general heuristics and production system methodology to accomplish pattern detection and the discovery of scientific laws. Among the classical laws rediscovered by BACON.3 is Kepler's third law of planetary motion. It must be emphasized that BACON.3's discoveries of scientific laws do not entail an explanation of the data; the laws only provide a summary of the data in the form of equations. In this section, BACON.3, developed by Langley (1981), will be described with respect to its major characteristics. An example of the system's behavior will be provided, a summary and analysis of BACON.3's discoveries will be presented, and a commentary on BACON.3's strengths and limitations will be offered.

Characteristics of BACON.3

In order to discover scientific laws, BACON.3 relies on a set of general heuristics that recast data and theoretical terms at increasingly abstract levels of description. The first set of these heuristics operates at the level of data collection. The functions of these data gathering productions are summarized in Section 1 of Table 5.1.

TABLE 5.1
Set of Productions in the BACON.3 System

1. Gathering Data

   The first set of 17 productions is responsible for gathering directly observable data. Of these productions, 7 are responsible for gathering information from the user about the task to be considered. This information consists of the names of all variables, along with suggested values for those variables under the system's control. Once this information has been gathered, the remaining 10 productions gather data through a standard factorial design.

   First the values of one independent term are varied while those of the others are held constant. Next, the value of the second variable is incremented and all values of the first are again considered under these conditions. This continues until all values of the second term have been generated. Now the value of the third variable is incremented, and the cycle begins again. In this manner, all combinations of independent variable values are eventually generated. The values of all dependent variables are observed for each combination.

2. Discovering Regularities

   The second set of 16 productions is responsible for noting regularities in the data collected by the first set. These rules can temporarily interrupt the data gathering productions while pursuing their own goals. The system's regularity detectors can be divided into a set of *constancy detectors* and a set of *trend detectors*. The first of these can deal with either symbolic or numerical data; they create higher level descriptive clusters by formulating generalizations and finding the conditions on them. BACON.3's trend detectors operate only on numerical data.

3. Calculating Theoretical Values

   Once a theoretical term has been defined at a given level, 3 additional productions calculate the values of this term for the clusters at that level. Since a theoretical term is tied to a particular level of description, the values of some terms are obtained only after considerable work has been done at lower levels. Once these values have been calculated, they are fair game for the regularity detectors, and new levels of description may be created and more complex theoretical terms may be defined. This results from the fact that defined terms are not distinguished from directly observable variables when noting regularities.

4. Noting Redundant Theoretical Terms

   Before calculating the values of a new theoretical term, BACON.3 must make sure that the term is not equivalent to an existing concept. If a redundant term's values were calculated, then mathematically valid but empirically uninteresting relationships (e.g., $x/x = 1$) could be detected. Accordingly, a fourth set of 22 productions decomposes new terms into their primitive components. If the definition of a new variable is identical to an existing definition, the term is rejected, and other relations are considered (or, in the case of a linear relationship, the new term is replaced by the old).

5. Ignoring Differences

Suppose BACON.3 has defined two intercept concepts. . . . The values of the first, intercept$_{pv,t,1}$ are 0 when the number of moles is 1, while the values of a second, intercept$_{pv,t,2}$ are 0 when the number of moles is 2. One would like BACON.3 to generalize at this point, stating that the intercept of *all* lines relating the pressure-volume to the temperature is 0, regardless of the number of moles. However, because the two intercepts are different terms, the constancy detector described above cannot be applied.

BACON.3's solution to this problem is to note the definitions of the two intercepts differ only by a constant coefficient, and to define an *abstraction* of the two which ignores this difference. Abstracted terms are tied to one level higher than the terms from which they are created; there is no need to rediscover a constancy that is already known, so the abstracted values are copied directly to the higher level clusters. Once these values have been copied, the regularity detectors can be applied, in this case, the value of the abstracted term is always 0.

6. Collapsing Clusters

When a constancy is noted, a higher level description is created and conditions are found for it. Later, if a constancy is observed on a different variable, a separate cluster is specified. If the two clusters have identical conditions, they are combined into a single structure; only 3 productions are devoted to this process. Once this has happened to a number of cluster pairs, the values of the dependent terms can be compared and regularities may emerge.

For example, suppose BACON.3 has run experiments with a pendulum at various locations and found that Galileo's pendulum law, $P^2/L = K$, holds at each location. In this equation, P is the period of the pendulum and L is the length of the support. However, suppose the value of K varies at each location. Now, imagine that BACON.3 drops a set of objects at each location, and finds that the acceleration of these objects also differs according to the location. Upon combining the information acquired at identical locations, a regularity is detected. Since the acceleration increases as the period^2/length increases, the product acceleration·period^2/length is considered; the value of this term is constant regardless of the location.

7. Handling Irrelevant Variables

Consider again Galileo's law for pendulums, and assume BACON.3 begins by varying the values for *four* independent variables — length of the support, the location of the experiment, the weight of the supported object, and the initial angle of the support with respect to the vertical. In fact, both the weight and the angle (if small values are examined) are *irrelevant* to the period of the pendulum, but this is not obvious from the outset.

To deal with such situations, BACON.3 draws on a set of 8 productions. The most important of these nodes clusters is the level in which the description for a variables value is *two more* than the level at which the variable was defined; this implies that the variable most recently varied has had no effect on the dependent values. The effect of this production is to modify the data gathering scheme so the value considered is used for the rest of the run. The remaining productions carry out the details of this process.

Table 5.1, continued

---

8. Summary of the Discovery Method
    In summary, BACON.3 gathers data in systematic fashion, varying one term at
    a time and observing its effects. If a variable has no effects, it is marked as
    irrelevant and its manipulation is abandoned. If one variable does influence
    another, a new theoretical term is defined, incorporating both the independent and
    the dependent variables. If this term has not been considered before, its values are
    computed and examined. When these values are constant, BACON.3 creates a
    new, higher level description which it treats as data on that level. The new cluster
    may be combined with others if it has identical conditions. When the values of the
    new term are not constant, it is used to define a more complex term and the process
    repeats. In addition, the search for useful theoretical terms and constancies occurs
    anew at each level of description. Taken together, these heuristics make BACON.3
    a powerful yet general discovery system.

Source: Langley, P. (1981). Data-driven discovery of physical laws. *Cognitive Science*,
5, 31–54. Reprinted with the permission of the Ablex Publishing Corporation.

In order to recast the collected data, BACON.3 applies a set of
heuristics that discerns patterns or regularities and leads to higher levels
of description. A summary of productions that detect regularities is given
in Section 2 of Table 5.1.

A third set of heuristics is devoted to the calculation of values of
theoretical terms at a given level of description. The process of calculating theoretical values is summarized in Section 3 of Table 5.1

A fourth set of productions is devoted to the detection of redundancies
of new theoretical terms with existing theoretical terms. This process of
redundancy detection is summarized in Section 4 of Table 5.1.

A fifth set of productions controls an abstraction process whereby
differences in theoretical terms can be ignored. This process of ignoring
differences and creating abstractions at higher levels of description is
summarized in Section 5 of Table 5.1.

A sixth set of productions is devoted to the process of combining
clusters that have identical conditions. This process of collapsing clusters
with identical conditions into single structures is summarized in Section
6 of Table 5.1.

A seventh set of productions is directed toward the detection of
irrelevant variables and to dropping their values from consideration. The
mechanisms for discovering irrelevant variables and controlling their
effects are summarized in Section 7 of Table 5.1.

The BACON.3 system depends on these seven sets of productions (86 productions in all) for the discovery of physical laws. The following subsection contains an example of BACON.3's discovery process: the discovery of a version of Kepler's third law of planetary motion.

BACON.3's Discovery of Kepler's Third Law

The general methodology of BACON.3, as discussed above and summarized in Table 5.1, was applied in the rediscovery of physical laws originally discovered by Kepler, Galileo, Ohm, and others. In the following account of an interesting approach to the rediscovery of Kepler's third law, material in brackets identifies the general set of heuristics (Table 5.1) used in various stages of the discovery process (Langley, 1981, pp. 40–42).

Kepler's third law relates a planet's distance from the sun to its period of revolution. The law also holds for other bodies with satellites, such as Jupiter, though the constant involved is different. The law may be stated as $d^3/p^2 = c$, where d is the distance from the central body, p is the period, and c is a constant. The levels of description approach suggests an interesting way to discover this law. Assume a simplified solar system in which all orbits are circular. This has two important implications. First, the distance between a satellite and the body it orbits is a constant over time. Second, it implies that equal fractions of a satellite's orbit are covered in equal times. This second point can be derived from Kepler's second law, that equal areas of an orbit are covered in equal times.

BACON.3 is given control [Section 1 of Table 5.1] over three observational variables — an origin object, a vector object, and the time at which this pair of objects is observed. Two dependent variables [Section 1 of Table 5.1] are used. One of these is the distance between the observed origin and vector objects. The second assumes a fixed coordinate such as a star, which is distant enough that motions within the solar system can be effectively ignored in computing angles with respect to it. (This is true of even the closest stars. Astronomers attempted to use the method of parallax to estimate stellar distances for over a century before their instruments were made sensitive enough to detect any motion.) BACON.3 is given access to the angle made using the fixed star and vector object as the end points, and using the origin object as the pivot point. BACON.3 begins by collecting [Section 1 of Table 5.1] values of these last two attributes for various pairs of solar objects at various times. [Table 5.2] shows some of the data gathered in this manner. The program quickly discovers [Section 2 of Table 5.1] that in some cases certain values for the distance recur. The conditions found [Section 2 of Table 5.1] for the resulting generalizations are that the origin object is the sun and that the vector object is one of the planets. A set of second-level descriptions are created [Section 2 of Table 5.1], describing these regularities.

TABLE 5.2
First Level Data of the Solar System

Origin	Vector	Time	Distance	Angle	Slope A,T
Sun	Mercury	50	0.38719	52.909	4.09090
Sun	Mercury	60	0.38719	52.909	4.09090
Sun	Mercury	70	0.38719	52.909	4.09090
Sun	Venus	50	0.72398	49.000	1.60000
Sun	Venus	60	0.72398	65.000	1.60000
Sun	Venus	70	0.72398	81.000	1.60000
Sun	Earth	50	1.00000	185.860	0.98563
Sun	Earth	60	1.00000	195.710	0.98563
Sun	Earth	70	1.00000	205.570	0.98563

Source: Langley, P. (1981). Data-driven discovery of physical laws. *Cognitive Science*, 5, 31–54. Reprinted with the permission of the Ablex Publishing Corporation.

Concurrently, BACON.3 notices [Section 2 of Table 5.1] that as the time increases, the angles seem to increase. (This assumes knowledge that this variable's values are cyclical, e.g., that $30° - 90° = 300°$.) In each case, the slope of the angle with respect to the time is a different constant. As a result, theoretical terms for the slopes and intercepts of these linear relations are defined [Section 2 of Table 5.1], with slightly different concepts being created to describe different lines. The conditions under which these relations hold are also found [Section 2 of Table 5.1]. The resulting clusters are presented in [Table 5.3].

TABLE 5.3
Second Level Data of the Solar System

Origin	Vector	Distance	Slope A,T	DS	D^2S	D^3S^2
Sun	Mercury	0.38719	4.090900	1.58400	0.61330	0.97146
Sun	Venus	0.72398	1.600000	1.15840	0.83864	0.97146
Sun	Earth	1.00000	0.985630	0.98563	0.98563	0.97146
Sun	Mars	1.52370	0.544020	0.79847	1.21670	0.97146
Sun	Jupiter	5.19910	0.083141	0.43226	2.24740	0.97146
Sun	Saturn	9.53850	0.033457	0.31913	3.04410	0.97146

Source: Langley, P. (1981). Data-driven discovery of physical laws. *Cognitive Science*, 5, 31–54. Reprinted with the permission of the Ablex Publishing Corporation.

Next, BACON.3 notices [Section 6 of Table 5.1] that it has a number of second-level clusters with identical sets of conditions, but with different generalizations. Accordingly, it collapses [Section 6 of Table 5.1] these clusters and places slopes, intercepts, and distances together. The next step in finding Kepler's third law is to relate the distances to the slope of the angles with respect to time. However, each slope is a different theoretical term, and in this form they cannot be compared with the distances.

First, BACON.3 must realize that each of these concepts' definitions differ only by a single numerical parameter, and that since it has just moved up a level of description, it might ignore [Section 5 of Table 5.1] these differences and treat these terms as identical. The parameters are no longer needed since the values of the slopes have already been calculated, so the program creates [Section 5 of Table 5.1] a new, more abstract variable for the slope of the angle with respect to the time, and replaces the old terms with this new one. A similar process is applied to the intercepts.

Now, BACON.3 has second level data it can examine, and immediately finds [Section 2 of Table 5.1] a monotonic decreasing relation between the distance d and the slope s. A new variable, ds, is defined [Section 2 of Table 5.1] and its values examined; now the system notes [Section 2 of Table 5.1] a decreasing relation between ds and the distance. Another term is created [Section 2 of Table 5.1]; d^2s and ds also seem inversely related; and once it [the term] is examined, yet another relation is found [Section 2 of Table 5.1]. The terms d^2s and ds also seem inversely related, so their product, d^3s^2, is defined as a new variable. This term is found to have a constant value, so a third level descriptive cluster is generated [Section 2 of Table 5.1]; in each case, the Sun is the origin object, so this is added [Section 2 of Table 5.1] as a condition to the rule.

Later, when BACON.3 considers a different set of objects, Jupiter and its satellites, these variables stand it in good stead. Rather than having to repeat the process, it simply calculates [Section 3 of Table 5.1] the values of existing concepts. Again the theoretical term d^3s^2 is found [Section 2 of Table 5.1] to be constant, but this time with a different value. The common aspect of these clusters is that Jupiter is the origin object, so this is added [Section 2 of Table 5.1] as a condition to this new third level descriptive cluster. Note that the values of s are inversely proportional to the planet's periods, so that d^3s^2 = .97146 is an alternate formulation of Kepler's third law.

Scientific Discoveries of BACON.3

In addition to the discovery of a version of Kepler's third law, BACON.3 discovered a number of other empirical laws. In this section, the empirical laws, their diversity, and their relative complexity will be discussed. The generality of BACON.3's methodology will be considered in two ways: the extent to which each of its seven sets of heuristics

(Table 5.1) was involved in the discoveries, and the effect of changing the order of the experiments that lead to the discoveries.

BACON.3 discovered five scientific laws: the ideal gas laws; Kepler's third law; Coulomb's law; Galileo's laws; and Ohm's law. The equations for these laws are presented in Table 5.4.

TABLE 5.4
Equations Discovered by BACON.3

Ideal gas law	$pV/nT = K_1$
Kepler's third law	$d^3[(a - k_2)/t]^2 = k_3$
Coulomb's law	$Fd^2/q_1q_2 = k_4$
Galileo's laws	$dP^2/Lt^2 = k_5$
Ohm's law	$D^2T/(LI + k_6D^2I) = K_7$

Source: Langley, P. (1981). Data-driven discovery of physical laws. *Cognitive Science*, 5, 31–54. Reprinted with the permission of the Ablex Publishing Corporation.

In the equation for the ideal gas laws, n is the quantity of gas (in moles), p is the pressure exerted in the gas, V is the volume of the gas, T is the temperature of the gas (in degrees Kelvin), and K_1 is a constant.

In the equation for Kepler's third law, the expression in brackets is the slope of the angle with respect to time (as described in the previous section), d is the distance of the planet (or satellite) from the Sun (or central body), and k_3 is a constant (.97146, as described in the previous section).

In the equation for Coulomb's law, F is the electrical force between two spheres (in a torsion balance), d is the initial distance between the two spheres, q_1 and q_2 are charges on the spheres, and k_4 is a constant (8.99×10^9 Newton-meters^2/Coulombs^2).

In the equation for Galileo's laws (the law of pendulum motion and the law of uniform acceleration), P is the period of the pendulum, L is the length of the support, d is the distance traversed after an object is dropped, t is the elapsed time after the object was dropped, and k_5 is a constant.

In the equation for Ohm's law, T is the temperature differential at the ends of a metal bar to which the ends of a copper wire are tapped, L is the length of the wire, D is the diameter of the wire, I is the current through the wire, and k_6 and k_7 are constants.

The empirical laws discovered by BACON.3 exhibit diversity in subject matter and in algebraic expression: from the laws of the solar system to the physics of motion, gases, and electricity; from the squaring of a ratio (Kepler's law) to simple ratios and products (ideal gas laws) to the ratio of squared variables (Galileo's laws).

The algebraic complexity of Ohm's law suggests computational complexity in its discovery. As compared with the other laws, the discovery of Ohm's law required a larger number of productions, a larger size of working memory, more levels of description, and more theoretical terms.

BACON.3's heuristics appear to be general across the set of five empirical laws. This generality held in the case of five sets of productions: factorial experimental design in the collection of data (Section 1 of Table 5.1), discovering the regularities (Section 2 of Table 5.1), calculating theoretical values (Section 3 of Table 5.1), noting redundant theoretical terms (Section 4 of Table 5.1), and collapsing clusters (Section 6 of Table 5.1). The heuristics involved in the development of abstractions by ignoring differences (Section 5 of Table 5.1) were used in the discovery of four of the laws (the discovery of Galileo's laws was the exception). The productions involved in the handling of irrelevant variables (Section 7 of Table 5.1) were used only for the discovery of Galileo's laws.

The generality of the BACON.3 system is indicated by its ability to arrive at the empirical laws by various orders or sequences of experimental observations. Variations in order could lengthen or shorten the time required to discover a law, but the identical law was still discovered. Computational complexity (for example, number of productions used, size of working memory) was an experimental order effect, but the attainment of the empirical law was not an experimental order effect.

Commentary on BACON.3

BACON.3 embodies a set of heuristics that perform, in machine fashion, intellective functions of induction, abstraction, generalization, factorial experimentation, and calculation. The machine executes these intellective functions under the guidance of its symbolic language.

The heuristic codes are, as indicated in the previous section, general in the sense that they can execute different content, but the heuristic codes are indifferent to and uncomprehending of the content. The comprehension lies with the human user of BACON.3. BACON.3 did not independently discover or rediscover any laws; it merely executed heuristic codes designed and interpreted by its developer.

BACON.3 produced equations that are descriptive and empirical. Its heuristics can, no doubt, be extended to other descriptive laws in physics and other domains (Langley et al., 1987). However, its heuristics are inadequate for theoretical conceptualization of the complex explanatory laws that constitute contemporary knowledge in such areas as nuclear physics.

In conclusion, BACON.3 is a machine representation of the inductive and Baconian (Francis Bacon, 1561–1626, a British philosopher of science) method of descriptive science. It remains to be seen whether artificial intelligence research (Caudill and Butler, 1990; Partridge and Wilkes, 1990) can develop machine representation (Kulkarni and Simon, 1988) of discovery in theoretical science (Wagman, 1991b, Chapter 4).

EXPERIMENTAL REDISCOVERY OF KEPLER'S THIRD LAW

General Logic of the Laboratory Replication

As discussed in the previous section of this chapter, the BACON.3 program employed systematic heuristics to rediscover by inductive or data driven procedures a number of physical science laws, including Kepler's third law of planetary motion. Qin and Simon (1990) conducted a laboratory experiment whose objective was to compare BACON's discovery heuristics with the heuristics of university students given the task of discovering the functional relationship between two sets of data that, unknown to the subjects, was equivalent to the data available to Kepler: for each of five planets (Mercury, Venus, Earth, Mars, Jupiter), its distance from and period of revolution around the sun. The function discovered by Kepler and rediscovered by BACON.3 and possibly to be discovered in a laboratory experiment by university students states that the ratio of planetary distance cubed to planetary period squared is a constant. Qin and Simon (1990), in two experiments, obtained the protocols of successful and unsuccessful university students and related their problem-solving heuristics to heuristics embodied in the BACON program. Qin and Simon's interesting research will be described, and the implications of their results will be discussed in a commentary section.

The First Experiment: Method, Materials, and Subjects

Subjects were given two sets of data, simply labeled as s and q. The meaning of s and q was not revealed to subjects, but, in fact, they referred to distances (s) and periods (q) of five planets (Table 5.5). The following experimental task instructions were provided to subjects:

TABLE 5.5

The Data Given to Subjects in Experiment 1

s	q
36.00	88.00
67.25	224.70
93.00	365.30
141.75	687.00
483.80	4,332.10

Note: s = Distance; q = Period of Revolution

Source: Qin, Y. and Simon, H. A. (1990). Laboratory replication of scientific discovery processes. *Cognitive Science*, *14*, 281–312. Reprinted with the permission of the Ablex Publishing Corporation.

We are interested in how a human being discovers a scientific law. This experiment is not designed to test your problem-solving ability. It is simply to discover what methods you would use to build a formula describing the relationship between two groups of given data.

In order to follow your thoughts we ask that you think aloud, explaining each step as thoroughly as you can.

The data will be presented on another sheet of paper, and you should begin by reading the data aloud [Qin and Simon, 1990, p. 283].

To discover the scientific formula, subjects (unlike Kepler, who discovered the planetary law in 1620) were permitted to use a modern calculator that computed mathematical functions.

The experiment generally lasted about one hour unless subjects solved the problem in a shorter time. Subjects were allowed to use pen, scratch paper, and a calculator that had multiplication and division operators as well as exponential and logarithmic functions [Qin and Simon, 1990, p. 283].

Qin and Simon provide the following information about the nine experimental subjects:

Nine subjects took part in Experiment 1. Their academic status is shown in Table [5.6]. Five were undergraduates, all of whom had taken or were taking courses in physics, calculus, and chemistry; one was a graduate student in physics, one an engineer, one a graduate student in art history, and one a graduate student in education [Qin and Simon, 1990, p. 283].

TABLE 5.6
Subjects and Their Best Results in Experiment 1

Subject	Situation	Best Results
S1	Sophomore	$s/q = c$, $s^2/q = c$, $s^{1.25} = q$
S2	Senior	$Inq/Ins = c$
S3	Freshman	$s^3/6.025 = q^2$ (correct)
S4	Junior EE	$s^{1.49} = q$ (nearly correct)
S5	Freshman	$88 - 2*36 = 16$ ($q_i = ks_ib$, $i = 1,2,3,4$)?
		$22^2 = 484$
SY	Graduate Student in Physics	$q^{2/3} = 0.55s$ (correct)
SW	Engineer	$s^2/q = c$, $s^3/q = c$
SG	Graduate Student in Art	$q_1/s_1 = x_1*y$
SG	History	$q_2/s_2 = x_2*y$
		$q_3/s_3 = x_3*y$
SJ	Graduate Student in Education	$q = 2^x*s+b$

Note: s = Distance; q = Period of Revolution

Source: Qin, Y. and Simon, H. A. (1990). Laboratory replication of scientific discovery processes. *Cognitive Science, 14*, 281–312. Reprinted with the permission of the Ablex Publishing Corporation.

General Results

Two subjects succeeded in discovering the formula. The protocol of a successful subject will be presented following a brief summary of general difficulties inherent in the problem and general characteristics of subject behavior.

The problem is marked by three types of difficulty:

1. The relation between q and s is nonlinear. Three subjects, S5, SG, and SJ, failed because they only tried linear relations. (Note that the latter two

subjects were the least sophisticated, mathematically, of the nine.) Other subjects, for example, SW, spent a great deal of their time in unsuccessful efforts to find a linear relation.

2. If we write the law in the form, $q = f(s)$, we get a nonintegral power of s, $3/2$. SW failed to solve the problem through not testing nonintegral powers, and S1 found no systematic way to arrive at the correct power.
3. The constant coefficient in the law is not unity. This was at the root of the failures of S1, S2, and S4, who neglected to include the coefficient in the functions they were considering [Qin and Simon, 1990, p. 286].

General characteristics of the search for the correct mathematical function are epitomized as follows:

Linear functions were considered most frequently. . . . Sequential functions are next most often considered, then quadratic functions, then logarithmic functions. *Simple functions were considered more frequently than complex ones.* . . . *There are large individual differences in the functions considered.* . . . *Diagrams were used extensively* [Qin and Simon, 1990, pp. 287–289].

Protocol of Successful Subject SY

The protocol of successful subject SY was assembled from both the subject's work product and the subject's thinking-aloud behavior.

1. You said don't use logarithm? Ok, try something else.
2. Try a simple function.
3. The simplest one is square, x square.
4. Check if their squares fit or not,
5. $88^{1/2} = 9.38$
6. $(36/4)^2 = 88$
7. $(67.25/4)^2 = 282$
8. The difference (between 282 and 224.7) is big.
9. Again, $(93/4)^2$ ...
10. No, it's wrong.
11. The difference is too big.
12. The square increases too fast.
13. So, try s^3 and q^2.
14. $36^3/88^2 = $ ... The easier way (using this calculator) is $88^{3/2} = 19.87$.
15. $88^{2/3}/36 = 0.54(96)$
16. $224.7^{2/3}/67.25 = 0.55$
17. $365^{2/3}/93 = 0.55$
18. $687^{2/3}/141.75 = 0.55$
19. It looks not bad
20. $4,332^{2/3}/483.8 = 0.55$

21. It seems that it is this kind of relationship.
22. E: Write it down.
23. S: That is, s cube is in direct ratio to q square [Qin and Simon, 1990, p. 289].

Characteristics of Successful and Unsuccessful Subjects

The results of the first experiment reveal major differences between successful and unsuccessful subjects.

All the subjects used heuristics like BACON's.

Heuristics 1, 2, and 3, were used by everyone. Heuristics 4 and 5 were also used frequently, although not to the same extent by all subjects. The successful subjects proceeded relatively systematically, and obtained relevant information by feedback from the search. The unsuccessful subjects were less systematic, and less able to obtain information from their tests of hypotheses. As a result, they were not able, systematically and successfully, to use Heuristics 4 and 5, which depend upon feedback [Qin and Simon, 1990, p. 296].

The Second Experiment

The second experiment introduced one change. Subjects were not provided with a calculator to compute exponential and logarithmic functions, thereby more nearly matching Kepler's computational resources. The expected result was that subjects took longer than subjects in the first experiment to discover Kepler's third law of planetary motion. Of the five subjects in the second experiment, two succeeded.

The general outcome of the second experiment was similar to the results of the first experiment: "Linear functions were considered most frequently, simple functions were considered more frequently than complex ones, there were large individual differences in the functions considered, and diagrams were used extensively" [Qin and Simon, 1990, p. 298].

Behavior of Successful Subjects

The problem-solving behavior of successful subjects is quite similar to that of the successful subjects in the first experiment: "They searched relatively systematically, obtained feedback from their tests of hypotheses, and used the feedback to guide further search" [Qin and Simon, 1990, p. 298].

The Data Manipulations of Successful Subject S8

S8's pattern of solution was highly efficient: Subject 8 manipulated the data, examining only a few functions, and found the law very quickly. . . . Most of the manipulations consisted in computing functions of s, then comparing these with q. S8 used Heuristic 4 in combination with hill-climbing search (successive approximation), and solved the problem without help of a diagram [Qin and Simon, 1990, p. 299].

The Search Behavior of Successful Subject S9

In solving the problem, subject S9 used a scatter diagram, several mathematical functions, and Heuristic 5. "Subject S9 selected linear and quadratic equations, then constructed a scatter diagram of the data. Next, S9 chose the function $q = as^3$. After observing the behavior of this function, S9 used Heuristic 5 to find the solution" [Qin and Simon, 1990, p. 299].

The Search Behavior of Unsuccessful Subject S7

In contrast to successful subjects, subject S7 failed because of his preference for complex mathematical functions.

S7 proceeded more systematically than S6 or S10 [two other unsuccessful subjects], and obtained feedback that was used to guide the search. S7 searched by selecting successive functions, but failed to solve the problem after having spent an hour and a half. S7 failed by not sufficiently exploring simple functions, but tried complex ones such as the hyperbola, and derivatives, and integrals [Qin and Simon, 1990, p. 299].

Subjects' Heuristics and BACON's Heuristics

BACON rediscovered Kepler's third planetary law by systematic application of recursive heuristics. BACON's program moves with relentless efficiency. BACON's mechanical recursive heuristics are only approached by the heuristics of the human subjects, as summarized in the following account:

BACON's heuristics were used frequently by the subjects, although some of the objects to which BACON's Heuristic 4 or 5 were applied (see [Table 5.7]), were different from those used by BACON. These heuristics were evoked in somewhat different ways by BACON and the subjects. BACON uses its heuristics recursively. . . . The human subjects were not as systematic in their use. Often after the successful subjects evoked one of these heuristics, they did not immediately follow up the result. Instead, they first tried some other heuristic before turning back to a new application of the BACON heuristics. Or, like S8, they sometimes combined hill-climbing with BACON's Heuristic 4. After using one of BACON's heuristics, unsuccessful subjects generally neither followed up immediately, nor returned to it later [Qin and Simon, 1990, p. 303].

TABLE 5.7

BACON.1's Rules for Noting Regularities

---

1. FIND-LAWS
    If you want to iterate through the values of independent term I,
        and you have iterated through all the values of I,
    then try to find laws for the dependent values you have recorded.
2. CONSTANT
    If you want to find laws,
        and the term D has value V in all data clusters,
    then infer that D always has value V.
3. LINEAR
    If you want to find laws,
        and you have recorded a set of values for the term X,
        and you have recorded a set of values for the term Y,
        and the values of X and Y are linearly related
        with slope M and intercept B,
    then infer that a linear relation exists between X and Y with slope M and intercept
        B.
4. INCREASING
    If you want to find laws,
        and you have recorded a set of values for the term X,
        and you have recorded a set of values for the term Y,
        and the absolute values of X increase,
            as the absolute values of Y increase,
    then consider the ratio of X and Y.
5. DECREASING
    If you want to find laws,
        and you have recorded a set of values for the term X,
        and you have recorded a set of values for the term Y,
        and the absolute values of X increase,
            as the absolute values of Y decrease,
        and these values are not linearly related,
    then consider the product of X and Y.

Source: Qin, Y. and Simon, H. A. (1990). Laboratory replication of scientific discovery processes. *Cognitive Science*, *14*, 281–312. Reprinted with the permission of the Ablex Publishing Corporation.

The behavior of the subjects in this experiment may be compared with the behavior of the BACON program when it is given the same task. Kepler's third law is only one of the laws rediscovered by BACON, and exercises only a subset of BACON.4's capacities. In trying to rediscover Kepler's third law, most human subjects need to generate and choose among different function types. BACON, because of its structure, need not do so. It carries out its search using only linear functions and ratios.

BACON's Heuristics 1, 2, and 3, are used by almost every subject in these experiments. Successful subjects also used procedures closely resembling Heuristics 4 and/or 5 successfully (Heuristic 4 being used more often than 5). Unsuccessful subjects used Heuristics 4 and 5 only very unsystematically, or used them inappropriately. The heuristics used by the subjects are perhaps more general and flexible than those incorporated in BACON: For the most part, they can be regarded as forms of means-ends analysis. Sometimes, they are too general to be effective, for example, "If a variable increases, try to decrease it; if it decreases, try to increase it" [Qin and Simon, 1990, p. 304].

Commentary

It is important to recognize that scientific or philosophical theory played no role in the discovery of Kepler's third law of planetary motion by the BACON program and by the university students. The discovery was an exercise in mathematical computation. Kepler, on the other hand, was motivated not only by the need for a descriptive mathematical law but also by an overwhelming need to find an explanation for the relationship between the variables of planetary period and planetary distance. Had he not been absorbed in theoretical and cosmological speculations for a period of two decades, he would have, more quickly and with less personal frustration, found and accepted the mathematical function that so elegantly captures the planetary data. The need to know why is a human need, and many great scientists following Kepler sought explanations for descriptive mathematical laws.

Maxwell formulated a theory of electromagnetism, but electrical fields and magnetic fields are fictions, and the knowledge we have of electromagnetism is embodied in Maxwell's partial differential equations. As Helmholtz said, "In Maxwell's theory an electric charge is but the recipient of a symbol" (quoted in Kline, 1985, p. 146). Indeed, much of current theoretical science consists of no more than mathematical symbols and mathematical equations.

The implication is that further development of intelligent systems of which BACON is a primitive example may accelerate the pace with which the knowledge of nature is captured by and represented in expanding set of mathematical functions that, yet, fail, somehow, to satisfy the human need to know why.

It is important to recognize that it was by means of inductive reasoning that the relationship between a planet's distance from the sun and its period of rotation was computed by university students in the Qin and Simon experiment, the BACON program, and Johannes Kepler. The discovered equation was, in each case, data driven. A mathematical derivation of the equation provides the certainty characteristic of deductive reasoning. This derivation can be accomplished from Newtonian laws of motion and gravitation. The challenge to cognitive science is to go beyond data-driven procedures such as those in the BACON program to theory-based procedures that would emulate mathematical derivation of Kepler's third law. The EUREKA program (Elio and Scharf, 1990) can use its stock of equations to solve problems in elementary kinematics and, as discussed elsewhere, may be capable of deriving Kepler's third law from its equations.

SCIENTIFIC DISCOVERY AND HUMAN INTELLECT

The Transformation of Scientific Concepts

The processes of scientific discovery are complex and dependent upon the achievement of a resolution of empirical and theoretical stringencies. The transformation and dissolution of conflicting stringencies depend on restructuring the configuration of the problem and its conflicting elements. There is, perhaps, no clearer example of this process of scientific discovery than that of the astronomer Johannes Kepler, who transformed the concept of circular planetary motion (Hanson, 1958). An additional reason for selecting Johannes Kepler is to permit a comparison of the intellectual processes involved in his astronomical discoveries with the machine processes involved in BACON.3's rediscovery of Kepler's third law (see the section on scientific discovery and artificial intelligence in this chapter). The comparison of scientific discovery processes in Kepler and BACON.3 will be presented later in this chapter (see the section on discovery and a general theory of intelligence).

Kepler's Transformation of the Concept of Circular Planetary Motion

During the two millenia preceding the scientific discoveries of Johannes Kepler (1571–1630), the Platonic analogy between the perfection of geometry and the perfection of the heavens commanded the absolute and universal allegiance of astronomers, philosophers, and theologians. The doctrine of circular planetary orbits operated as a conceptual ligature in Kepler's scientific investigations. Thus, as will be detailed below, Kepler developed a sound method (equal areas in equal times) and sound reasoning concerning the orbit of the planet Mars but came to mistrust and abandon, for a time, both his method and reasoning when they led to the conclusion that the orbit of Mars could not be circular.

In a treatise of more than 300 pages, entitled *De Motibus Stellae Martis* (1937), Kepler presented a detailed account of his investigations concerning the orbit of Mars and the nature of the solar system. *De Motibus Stellae Martis* contains Kepler's complex reasoning, his perplexities, his attempts to reconcile theory and data, his many hypotheses, misconceptions, and errors, and, after years of work, his culminating discoveries elegantly set forth in three laws of the solar system.

From Geocentrism to Heliocentrism

In the early chapters of *De Motibus Stellae Martis*, Kepler presents an account of his discussions with his fellow astronomer Tycho Brahe. These discussions were held in Prague in 1600 and concerned Brahe's theory of the orbit of Mars. The theory included the postulates of geocentrism and of circular planetary motion. Kepler could not accept Brahe's theory, which, under the postulate of geocentrism, led to discrepancies of as much as five degrees of arc with observations. Kepler replaced the geocentrism postulate with a heliocentrism hypothesis on the basis that the Sun's huge magnitude compared with any of the planets and its centrist location in the planetary system probably determine the character of planetary motion.

Whereas Brahe's geocentrism postulate led him to study first the orbit of Mars (in his theory, there is no terrestrial orbit), Kepler's heliocentrism hypothesis led him to study first the orbit of the Earth.

From Circular Orbit to Noncircular Orbit

Kepler applied the method of equal angles in equal times (or equal areas in equal times) to his studies of the orbit of Mars. However, as detailed in *De Motibus Stellae Martis*, under the postulate that the orbit of Mars was circular (see discussion above of the two-millennia belief in the doctrine of circular planetary motion), the method of equal areas in equal times produced errors of plus or minus eight minutes of arc deviation from observations. Kepler responded to these stringencies among the observations, the postulate of circular orbit, and the method of equal areas by protracted self-debate as to which would have to be given up — the circular orbit postulate or the equal areas method: "From which it is shown what I promise to do in chapters XX, XXII . . . that the planet's orbit is not a circle but has the figure of an oval" (Kepler, quoted in Hanson, 1958, p. 75).

As indicated in *De Motibus Stellae Martis*, Kepler then proceeds to reject his own conclusion that the orbit is not circular and reaches, instead, the conclusion that his method of areas is incorrect:

Given that the orbit is circular, and supposing my reasoning to be correct, then the observations α, β, γ, are directly predicted; but α, β, γ do not occur; *therefore my reasoning was not correct.* After failing to reconcile the circular orbit with the equations given by the method of areas, he actually abandoned *the latter*. Different considerations were required to convince him that it was the circular orbit hypothesis that was ruining his theory. Only when the distances given to him by the circle were repeatedly inconsistent with those observed by Tycho, did Kepler begin systematically to doubt the circular orbit hypothesis. Even then he headed the next chapter "De Causis Naturalibus Hujas Deflexionis Planetae a Circulo" [Hanson, 1958, p. 76].

From Ovoid Orbit to Elliptical Orbit

After Kepler had finally and resolutely decided that the orbit of Mars was not circular, his next self-debate turned on the question of the specific nature of the noncircular orbital curve:

Whichever of these ways is used to describe the line on which the planet moves, it follows that this path, indicated by the following points, β, μ, α, δ, π, ρ, λ, is ovular, and not elliptical; to the latter, Mechanicians wrongly give the name derived from ovo. The egg (ovum) can be spun on two vertices, one flatter (obtuse), one sharper (acute). Further it is bound by inclined sides. This is the figure I have created.

All of this conspires to show that the resegmentum of our eccentric circle is much larger below than above, in equal recession from the apsides. Anyone can establish this either by numerical calculation or by mechanical drawing — some eccentricity being assumed [Kepler, quoted in Hall, 1955, p. 295].

Although Kepler was to arrive eventually at the ellipse as the correct noncircular curve, at this point in his thinking, the curve is clearly oviform or an ovoid.

Kepler now became concerned with creating a physical explanation for the physical oviform motion of Mars. He arrived at the explanatory hypothesis that the oviform orbit was the resultant of two attractive physical forces, one emanating from the Sun and one emanating from Mars.

However, the peculiar geometric properties of the oviform presented computational problems to Kepler, and he began to entertain the possibility that the orbit was a perfect ellipse. Once more, conceptual and empirical stringencies resulted in difficulties for Kepler. On the one hand, the oviform (as in the case of the circle) has but one focus. On the other hand, the geometric difficulties of the oviform could be relaxed if it were made to approximate an ellipse, but an ellipse has two foci. The required restructuring of his geometric model and reasoning preoccupied Kepler for some time. Ultimately, he was able to fit his physical data concerning the orbital motion of Mars to the mathematical properties of a perfect ellipse, with the Sun in one of the foci.

The enormous heap of calculations, velocities, positions and distances which had set Kepler his problem now pulled together into a geometrically intelligible pattern. The elliptical areas were seen to be equivalent; similarly, equations following from the ellipse were general expressions of Tycho's original data. All this made it clear that Mars revolved around the sun in an ellipse, describing around the sun areas proportional to its times of passage [Hanson, 1958, p. 83].

The Laws of the Solar System

Kepler then reasoned that, because the physical forces controlling the motion of the planet Mars operated throughout the solar system, the orbits of the other planets would also fit the mathematical model of the ellipse, obey the principle of equal areas in equal times, and have periods of revolution about the Sun and distances from the Sun in the ratio of p^2/d^3. These laws are presented in more detail in Table 5.8. The extraordinary astronomical discoveries of Johannes Kepler required two decades to completely revolutionize astronomical paradigm and dogma that had dominated conceptions of the solar system for two millennia.

TABLE 5.8

Kepler's Scientific Discoveries

---

1. Planetary orbits are elliptical with the sun in their common focus (1609).
2. They describe around the sun areas proportional to their times of passage (1609).
3. The squares of the time of their revolutions are proportional to the cubes of their greater axes, or their mean distances from the sun (1619).

Source: Hanson, N. R. (1958). *Patterns of discovery: An inquiry into the conceptual foundations of science*, p. 84. Cambridge: Cambridge University Press.

DISCOVERY AND A GENERAL THEORY OF INTELLIGENCE

The previous sections of this chapter have presented two approaches to scientific and mathematical discovery. The artificial intelligence approach was illustrated by the BACON.3 program. The human intellect approach was exemplified by Kepler's astronomical work. The purpose of the present section is to identify commonalities and differences in the two approaches.

Discovery and Inductive Logic

Inductive logic is well-represented in artificial intelligence research (Osherson and Smith, 1982) concerned with discovery and learning (Larkin et al, 1988). The LEX program (Mitchell, Utgoff, & Banerji, 1983) learns symbolic integration by generalizing and specializing among examples in a version space. The AM program (Lenat, 1976) uses inductive logic in generalizing and specializing numerical examples and relationships in order to discover conjectures and concepts in elementary number theory. The BACON.3 program (see the section on scientific discovery and artificial intelligence in this chapter) uses inductive logic in its data-driven detection of regularities and abstractions to discover or rediscover empirical laws in astronomy and physics.

The discovery of the laws of the solar system by Johannes Kepler and their rediscovery (Kepler's third law, in particular) by BACON.3 demonstrate essential identity as products in the form of equations. However, the processes of discovery are essentially disparate. BACON.3 obeyed its rules, performed its calculations, developed its abstractions, detected its regularities, and determined invariants in the ratios of variables, all in mechanical accordance with general heuristics (applicable to other domains of physical science as well), and generally followed a rigid inductive logic. In contrast, Kepler struggled to resolve theoretical and empirical constraints, to surmount his deep belief in the circularity of planetary motion, to reconcile conflicts involving his method of equal areas in equal times with the proper mathematical curve, to propose and reject numerous hypotheses, and to create an integrated theory that unified physical explanation and mathematical description of the motion of the planets and of the solar system.

Theoretical Science and Inductive Logic

The field of artificial intelligence has been neither a theoretical science nor a mathematical science (Simon, 1979) but, rather, an applied inductive science. This is especially clear in the case of BACON.3, in which heuristics are used to carry out inductive experiments that may lead to the establishment of regularities among independent and dependent variables. The regularities established are data driven rather than theory driven. The discoveries take the form of empirical functional relationships among variables. The laws discovered by BACON.3 are expressed as equations, but having been derived by inductive logic alone, the explanation of the laws, that is, their possible embodiment in a wider net of theory, is completely absent. BACON.3 is mechanism, not mind (Boden, 1988, 1990; Newell, 1990; Rychlak, 1990; Simon, 1990; Wagman, 1991b). Even the human mind, when relying solely on inductive logic, cannot develop theoretical science: "There is no inductive method which could lead to the fundamental concepts of physics. . . . In error are those theorists who believe that theory comes inductively from experience" (Einstein, 1933).

In the scientific era following Einstein, the technology of computers and artificial intelligence developed with applications ramifying throughout the natural sciences. These ramifications include theoretical physics as enthusiastically specified by Stephen Hawkins, one of the most eminent theoretical physicists of the last quarter of the twentieth century:

At present computers are a useful aid in research but they have to be directed by human minds. However, if one extrapolates their recent rapid rate of development, it would seem quite possible that they will take over altogether in theoretical physics. So maybe the end is in sight for theoretical physicists if not for theoretical physics [Hawkins, quoted in Davis and Hersh, 1986, p. 158].

The nature of human intellect is discoverable, the mathematics of human intellect is describable, and the computational representation of human intellect is constructible. A general unified theory of human and artificial intelligence can evolve.

Appendix

PARAMETERS AND PARADIGMS OF INFORMATION PROCESSING

The major parameters of information processing are presented in Table A.1. The major paradigms of information processing are presented in Table A.2.

TABLE A.1
Major Parameters for Information Processing

I. Information processes are decomposable into a logical structure of stages and substages.
II. Information transmission occurs in a forward time flow.
III. Information processing operations occur in finite time intervals.
IV. Information processing has a physical system locus.
V. Attributes of information processing stages
    A. Representations
        1. Input
        2. Output
        3. Discrete
        4. Continuous
    B. Processes
        1. Transmission
        2. Transformation
        3. Discrete
        4. Continuous
        5. Serial
        6. Parallel

TABLE A.2
Major Paradigms for Information Processing

Paradigms	References
Symbolic	Newell and Simon (1972)
	Newell (1990)
	Simon (1990)
Connectionist	Rumelhart and McClelland (1986)
	Smolensky (1988)
	Holland et al. (1986)
Unified symbolic-connectionist	Holyoak (1991)
	Holyoak and Thagard (1989)
	Thagard (1989, 1992)
	Shastri and Ajjangadde (1993)

GENERAL METHODS OF STUDYING MIND AND INTELLIGENCE

The sciences of cognition use different methods in studying the nature of mind and intelligence. Table A.3 lists the major approaches.

TABLE A.3
Major Approaches in the Study of Mind and Intelligence

Straight neuroscience, studying neurons or sections of the brain
Computational models of actual neurons in the brain
Connectionist models using distributed representations, so that a concept or hypothesis is a pattern of activation over multiple units
Connectionist models using localist representations, in which a single unit represents a concept or proposition
Traditional artificial intelligence models using data structures such as frames and production rules
Psychological experiments
Mathematical analysis
Theoretical speculation

Source: Thagard, P. (1989). Explanatory coherence. *Behavioral and Brain Sciences*, *12*, 457.

FUNDAMENTAL ELECTRONICS
OF THE DIGITAL COMPUTER

Information representation and processing in a computer depends on the logic of digit codes and the electronics of transistors. Keyes (1993) presents a brief and lucid description of the electronic fundamentals in the following account.

Digital computers operate by manipulating statements made in a binary code, which consists of ones and zeroes. A field-effect transistor is operated so that, like a relay, it is switched only "on" or "off." The device therefore represents exactly one binary unit of information: a bit. In a large-scale system, input signals control transistors, establishing connections that produce signals on output wires. The wires carry the signals to other switches that produce outputs, which are again sent on to another stage. The connections within the computer and the way in which the input signals determine an output together represent a logical statement. A series of such statements, in turn, determines a word in a document or an entry in a spreadsheet.

The field-effect transistor contains a channel that interacts with three electrodes: a source, which supplies electrons to the channel; a drain, which receives them at the other side; and a gate, which influences the conductivity of the channel. . . . Each part contains different impurity atoms, or dopants, which modify the electrical properties of the silicon.

The gate switches the transistor on when a positive voltage applied to it attracts electrons to the interface between the semiconductor and the gate insulator. These electrons then establish a connection between the source and drain electrodes that allows current to be passed between them. At this point, the transistor is "on." The connection persists for as long as the positive charge remains on the gate. An incoming signal is applied to the gate and, thus, determines whether the connection between source and drain is established. If a connection results, the output is connected to the ground potential, one of the standard digital voltages. If no connection results, the output is connected through the resistor to the positive power supply, the other standard digital voltage [Keyes, R. W. (1993). The future of the transistor. *Scientific American*, *268*, 70–78. Copyright © 1993 by Scientific American, Inc. All rights reserved].

FUZZY LOGIC AND ARTIFICIAL INTELLIGENCE

Fuzzy logic theory and applications became significant in artificial intelligence domains during the final decades of the twentieth century (Kosko, 1991; Zadeh, 1979). Applications include industrial and consumer devices, biological and economic research, and medical and financial information services. Fuzzy logic is a multivalued logic responsive to the imprecise character of human experience, judgment, and reasoning.

ABSTRACT TRANSFORMATIONS OF KNOWLEDGE

At an abstract level, advancement in human knowledge can be represented in terms of three types of transformations. In mathematics and mathematical philosophy, there are the transformations of order and chaos. In the physical world, there are the transformations of science and common sense. In the world of cognition, there are the transformations of computation and psychology. Table A.4 organizes these transformations of knowledge, with a brief remark about each.

TABLE A.4
Abstract Transformations of Knowledge

Transformations	Remarks
I. Mathematics and mathematical philosophy	I. Mathematics and mathematical philosophy
A. Chaos → chaos	A. Before the development of mathematics
B. Chaos → order	B. Mathematical conjecture
C. Order → chaos	C. Entropy
D. Order → order	D. Mathematical proof
II. Physical world	II. Physical world
A. Common sense → common sense	A. Naive physics
B. Common sense → science	B. Historical development of science
C. Science → common sense	C. Superstition
D. Science → science	D. Theory formulation and experimental validation
III. The world of cognition	III. The world of cognition
A. Psychology → psychology	A. Personal consciousness
B. Psychology → computation	B. Modeling of thought
C. Computation → psychology	C. Cognitive science explains thinking
D. Computation → computation	D. Computer thinking matches or surpasses human thinking

Bibliography

Alba, J. W. and Hasher, L. (1983). Is memory schematic? *Psychological Bulletin, 93*, 203–231.

Anderson, J. R. (1983). *The architecture of cognition.* Cambridge, MA: Harvard University Press.

Anderson, J. R., Farrell, R. and Sauers, R. (1984). Learning to program in LISP. *Cognitive Science, 8*, 87–129.

Appel, K. and Haken, W. (1979). The four color problem. In L. A. Steen (Ed.), *Mathematics today: Twelve informal essays* (pp. 153–180). New York: Springer-Verlag.

Barsalou, L. W. (1992). *Cognitive psychology: An overview for cognitive scientists.* Hillsdale, NJ: Lawrence Erlbaum Associates.

Bartlett, F. C. (1932). *Remembering: A study in experimental and social psychology.* Cambridge: Cambridge University Press.

Becker, J. D. (1973). A model for the encoding of experimental information. In R. C. Schank and K. M. Colby (Eds.), *Computer models of thought and language* (pp. 396–435). San Francisco, CA: Freeman.

Berry, D. C. (1983). Metacognitive experiences and transfer of logical reasoning. *Quarterly Journal of Experimental Psychology, 35A*, 39–49.

Birnbaum, L. (1991). Rigor mortis: A response to Nilsson's "Logic of artificial intelligence." *Artificial Intelligence, 47*, 57–77.

Boden, M. A. (1988). *Computer models of mind.* Cambridge: Cambridge University Press.

____. (1990). *The philosophy of artificial intelligence.* Oxford: Oxford University Press.

Bower, G. H., Black, J. B. and Turner, T. J. (1979). Scripts in memory for text. *Cognitive Psychology, 11*, 177–220.

Bradshaw, G. L. and Anderson, J. R. (1982). Elaborative encoding as an explanation of levels of processing. *Journal of Verbal Learning and Verbal Behavior, 21*, 165–174.

Braine, M. D. S. (1978). On the relation between the natural logic of reasoning and standard logic. *Psychological Review, 85*, 1–21.

Braine, M. D. S., Reiser, B. J. and Rumain, B. (1984). Some empirical justification for a theory of natural propositional logic. In G. H. Bower (Ed.), *The psychology of learning and motivation* (Vol. 18, pp. 313–371). New York: Academic Press.

Brooks, R. A. (1991). Intelligence without representation. *Artificial Intelligence, 47*, 57–77.

Brown, A. L. and Campione, J. C. (1985). Three faces of transfer: Implications for early competence, individual differences, and instruction. In M. Lamb, A. L. Brown and B. Rogoff (Eds.), *Advances in developmental psychology*. Hillsdale, NJ: Erlbaum.

Brown, R. (1977). *Use of analogy to achieve new expertise*. Unpublished Ph.D. dissertation, Massachusetts Institute of Technology, Cambridge, MA.

Burstein, M. H. (1983). Concept formation by incremental analogical reasoning and debugging. In *Proceedings International Machine Learning Workshop* (pp. 19–25). Monticello, IL.

____. (1986). Concept formation by incremental analogical reasoning and debugging. In R. S. Michalski, J. G. Carbonell and T. M. Mitchell (Eds.), *Machine learning: An artificial intelligence approach* (pp. 351–370). Los Altos, CA: Morgan Kaufmann.

Burnstein, M. and Adelson, B. (1987). Analogical learning: Mapping and integrating partial mental models. In *Program of the Ninth Annual Conference of the Cognitive Science Society*. Hillsdale, NJ: Erlbaum.

Carbonell, J. G. (1981). Invariance hierarchies in metaphor interpretation. *Proceedings Third Annual Meeting of the Cognitive Science Society*, Berkeley, CA.

____. (1982). Metaphor: An inescapable phenomenon in natural-language comprehension. In W. G. Lehnert and M. H. Ringle (Eds.), *Strategies for natural language processing* (pp. 415–435). Hillsdale, NJ: Erlbaum.

____. (1983a). Learning by analogy: Formulating and generalizing plans from past experience. In R. S. Michalski, J. G. Carbonell and T. M. Mitchell (Eds.), *Machine learning: An artificial intelligence approach* (pp. 137–162). Palo Alto, CA: Tioga.

____. (1983b). Derivational analogy in problem solving and knowledge acquisition. In *Proceedings International Machine Learning Workshop* (pp. 12–18). Monticello, IL.

____. (1986). Derivational analogy: A theory of reconstructive solving and expertise acquisition. In R. S. Michalski, J. G. Carbonell and T. M. Mitchell (Eds.), *Machine learning: An artificial intelligence approach* (pp. 371–392). Los Altos, CA: Morgan Kaufmann.

Carey, S. (1985). *Conceptual change in childhood*. Cambridge, MA: MIT Press/Bradford Books.

Caudill, M. and Butler, C. (1990). *Naturally intelligent systems*. Cambridge, MA: MIT Press.

Chang, C. L. and Lee, R. C. T. (1973). *Symbolic logic and mechanical memory*. Hillsdale, NJ: Erlbaum.

Chapman, D. (1987). Planning for conjunctive goals. *Artificial Intelligence, 32,* 333–377.

Chase, W. G. and Simon, H. A. (1973). Perception in chess. *Cognitive Psychology, 4,* 55–81.

Cheng, P. W. and Holyoak, K. J. (1985). Pragmatic reasoning schemas. *Cognitive Psychology, 17,* 391–416.

Cheng, P. W., Holyoak, K. J., Nisbett, R. E. and Oliver, L. M. (1986). Pragmatic versus syntactic approaches to training deductive reasoning. *Cognitive Psychology, 18,* 293–328.

Cheng, P. W. and Juang, J. (1987). A parallel resolution procedure based on connection graph. In *Proceedings AAAI-87,* Los Altos, CA.

Cheng, P. W. and Novick, L. R. (1990a). Where is the bias in causal attribution? In K. Gilhooly, M. Keane, R. Logre and G. Erdos (Eds.), *Line of thought: Reflections on the psychology of thinking* (pp. 181–197). Chichester: Wiley.

____. (1990b). A probabilistic contrast model of causal induction. *Journal of Personality and Social Psychology, 58,* 545–567.

____. (1991). Causes versus enabling conditions. *Cognition, 40,* 83–120.

Chomsky, N. (1956). *Knowledge of language: Its nature, origin, and use.* New York: Praeger.

____. (1981). *Lectures on government and binding.* Dordrecht, Netherlands: Foris Publications.

Chrostowski, J. J. and Griggs, R. A. (1983). The effects of problem content, instructions, and verbalization procedure on Wason's selection task. *Current Psychological Research and Reviews, 4,* 99–107.

Church, A. (1956). *Introduction to mathematical logic.* Princeton, NJ: Princeton University Press.

Clark, H. H. and Chase, W. G. (1972). On the process of comparing sentences against pictures. *Cognitive Psychology, 3,* 472–517.

Clement, C. and Gentner, D. (1991). Systematicity as a selection constraint in analogical mapping. *Cognitive Science, 15,* 89–132.

Clement, J. (1983a). A conceptual model discussed by Galileo and used intuitively by physics students. In A. Stevens and D. Gentner (Eds.), *Mental models.* Hillsdale, NJ: Erlbaum.

____. (1983b). Observed methods for generating analogies in scientific problem solving. In *Proceedings Annual Meeting of the American Educational Research Association,* Montreal, Quebec.

Clocksin, W. F. and Mellish, C. S. (1981). *Programming in PROLOG.* Berlin: Springer-Verlag.

Cox, J. P. and Griggs, R. A. (1982). The effect of experience on performance in Wason's selection task. *Memory and Cognition, 10,* 496–502.

Davis, P. J. and Hersh, R. (1986). *Descartes' dream: The world according to mathematics.* San Diego, CA: Harcourt Brace Jovanovich.

DeJong, G. and Mooney, R. J. (1986). Explanation-based learning: An alternative view. *Machine Learning, 1,* 145–176.

Descartes, R. (1951). *Meditation on first philosophy* (L. J. Lafleur, Trans.). New York: Library on Liberal Arts, Liberal Arts Press. (Original work published in 1641.)

Dietterich, T. G. (1986). Learning at the knowledge level. *Machine Learning, 1,* 287–315.

Doyle, J. (1980). *A model for deliberation, action, and introspection.* (AI TR-581). Cambridge, MA: MIT Artificial Intelligence Laboratory.

Dreyfus, H. L. (1972). *What computers can't do.* New York: Harper & Row.

Dyer, M. G. (1983a). *In-depth understanding.* Cambridge, MA: MIT Press.

____. (1983b). Understanding stories through morals and remindings. In *Proceedings IJCAI-83*, Washington, D.C.

____. (1991). Symbolic neuroengineering for natural language processing: A multilevel research approach. In J. Barnden and J. Pollack (Eds.), *Advances in connectionist and neural computation theory: Vol. 1: High level connectionist models* (pp. 32–86). Norwood, NJ: Ablex.

Ebbinghaus, H. (1885). *Uber das Gedachtnis.* Leipzig: Dunker & Humblot.

Eddington, A. S. (1933). *The nature of the physical world.* New York: Macmillan.

Einstein, A. (1931). *Essays in science.* New York: Philosophical Library.

____. (1933). *The method of theoretical physics.* New York: Oxford University Press.

Elio, R. and Scharf, P. (1990). Modeling novice-to-expert shifts in problem solving strategy and knowledge organization. *Cognitive Science, 14,* 576–639.

Etzioni, O. and Mitchell, T. M. (1989). A comparative analysis of chunking and decision analytic control. In *Proceedings AAAI Spring Symposium on Limited Rationality and AI,* Stanford, CA.

Evans, J. St. B. T. (1982). *The psychology of deductive reasoning.* London: Routledge and Kegan Paul.

Evans, T. G. (1968). A program for the solution of a class of geometric analogy intelligence test questions. In M. Minsky (Ed.), *Semantic information processing* (pp. 271–353). Cambridge, MA: MIT Press.

Falkenhainer, B., Forbus, K. D. and Gentner, D. (1986). The structure-mapping engine. In *Proceedings AAAI-86* (pp. 272–277). Philadelphia, PA.

Feigenbaum, E. A. and Simon, H. A. (1984). Epam-like models of recognition and learning. *Cognitive Science, 8,* 305–336.

Fisher, D. H. and Langley, P. (1985). Approaches to conceptual clustering. In *Proceedings IJCAI-85* (pp. 691–697). Los Angeles, CA.

Flynn, R. (1988). Placing SOAR on the connection machine, prepared for and distributed at the AAAI Mini-Symposium "How can slow components think so fast." Ann Arbor, MI.

Fodor, J. A. (1983). *The modularity of mind.* Cambridge, MA: Bradford Books/MIT Press.

Fodor, J. A. and Pylyshyn, Z. W. (1988). Connectionism and cognitive architecture: A critical analysis. *Cognition, 28,* 3–71.

Gasser, L. (1991). Social conceptions of knowledge and action: DAI foundations and open systems semantics. *Artificial Intelligence, 47,* 107–138.

Genesereth, M. R. (1983). An overview of meta-level architecture. *Proceedings AAAI-83* (pp. 119–124). Washington, D.C.

Genesereth, M. and Nilsson, N. (1987). *The logical foundations of artificial intelligence.* Los Altos, CA: Morgan Kaufmann.

Gentner, D. (1983). Structure-mapping: A theoretical framework for analogy. *Cognitive Science, 7,* 155–170.

____. (1987). Analogical inference and analogical access. In A. Prieditis (Ed.), *Analogica: The first workshop on analogical reasoning.* London: Pitman.

Gentner, D. and Gentner, D. (1983). Flowing waters or teeming crowds: Mental models of electricity. In A. Stevens and D. Gentner (Eds.), *Mental models*. Hillsdale, NJ: Erlbaum.

Gentner, D. and Jeziorski, M. (1989). Historical shifts in the use of analogy of science. In B. Gholson, W. R. Shadish, R. A. Neimeyer and A. Houts (Eds.), *Psychology of science: Contributions to metascience*. New York: Cambridge University Press.

Gentner, D. and Toupin, C. (1986). Systematicity and surface similarity in the development of analogy. *Cognitive Science, 10*, 277–300.

Gentzen, G. (1969). Investigations into logical deduction. In M. E. Szabo (Ed.), *The collected papers of Gerhard Gentzen* (pp. 68–131). (Originally uber das logische schliessen. *Mathematische Zeitschrift, 39*, 176–210, 405–431.)

Gholson, B., Eymard, L. A., Long, D., Morgan, D. and Leeming, F. C. (1988). Problem solving, recall, isomorphic transfer, and non-isomorphic transfer among third-grade and fourth-grade children. *Cognitive Development, 3*, 37–53.

Gibson, J. J. (1979). *The ecological approach to visual perception*. Boston: Houghton Mifflin.

Gick, M. L. and Holyoak, K. J. (1980). Analogical problem solving. *Cognitive Psychology, 12*, 306–355.

Glass, A. L. and Holyoak, K. J. (1975). Alternative conceptions of semantic memory. *Cognition, 3*, 313–339.

Gödel, K. (1930). Die Vollständigkeit der axiome des logischen funktionenkaküls. *Monatshefte für Matheematik und Physik, 37*, 349–360.

_____. (1931). Uber formal unentscheidbare satz de principia mathematica und verwandter system, I. *Monatshefte fur Mathematica und Physics, 13*, 173–189.

Greiner, R. (1985). Learning by understanding analogies. Ph.D. dissertation, Tech. Rept. STAN-CS-85-1071, Stanford University.

_____. (1988). Learning by understanding analogies. *Artificial Intelligence, 35*, 81–125.

Griggs, R. A. and Cox, J. R. (1982). The elusive thematic-materials effect in Wason's selection task. *British Journal of Psychology, 73*, 407–420.

Gupta, A. and Tambe, M. (1988). Suitability of message passing computers for implementing production systems. In *Proceedings AAAI-88* (pp. 687–692). St. Paul, MN.

Halford, G. S. and Wilson, W. H. (1980). A category theory approach to cognitive development. *Cognitive Psychology, 12*, 356–441.

Halford, G. S., Wilson, W. H., Guo, J., Wiles, J. and Stewart, J. E. M. (1993). Connectionist implications for processing capacity limitations in analogies. In K. J. Holyoak and J. A. Barnden (Eds.), *Advances in connectionist and neural computation theory: Vol. 2: Analogical connections*. Norwood, NJ: Ablex.

Hall, A. R. (1955). *The scientific revolution*. London: Longmans, Green and Co.

Hall, R. P. (1989). Computational approaches to analogical reasoning: A comparative analysis. *Artificial Intelligence, 39*, 39–120.

Hampton, J. A. (1982). A demonstration of intransitivity in natural concepts. *Cognition, 12*, 151–164.

_____. (1987). Inheritance of attributes in natural concept conjunctions. *Memory & Cognition, 15*, 55–71.

_____. (1988). Overextension of conjunctive concepts: Evidence for a unitary model of concept typicality and class inclusion. *Journal of Experimental Psychology:*

Learning, Memory and Cognition, 14, 12–32.

Hanson, N. R. (1958). *Patterns of discovery: An inquiry into the conceptual foundations of science.* Cambridge: Cambridge University Press.

Hayes, P. J. (1985). The second naive physics manifesto. In J. C. Hobbes and R. C. Moore (Eds.), *Formal theories of the commons world.* Norwood, NJ: Ablex.

Hayes-Roth, F. (1978). The role of partial and best matches in knowledge systems. In D. A. Waterman and F. Hayes-Roth (Eds.), *Pattern-directed inference systems* (pp. 557–576). New York: Academic Press.

Hesse, M. B. (1963). Models and analogies in science. In M. A. Hoskin (Ed.), *Newman history and philosophy of science series 14.* London: Sheed and Ward.

Hewitt, C. (1991). Open information systems semantics for distributed artificial intelligence. *Artificial Intelligence, 47*, 79–106.

Hillis, W. D. (1985). *The connection machine.* Cambridge, MA: MIT Press.

Hobbes, T. (1651). Leviathon. In Sir William Molesworth (Ed.), (1839–1945). *The English works of Thomas Hobbes of Mathersbury, 3.* London: John Bohn.

Hobbs, J. R. (1983a). Metaphor interpretation as selective inferencing: Cognitive processes in understanding metaphor (Part 1). *Empirical Studies of the Arts, 1*, 17–33.

____. (1983b). Metaphor interpretation as selective inferencing: Cognitive processes in understanding metaphor (Part 2). *Empirical Studies of the Arts, 1*, 125–142.

Hobbs, J. R. and Moore, R. (Eds.) (1985). *Formal theories of the commonsense world.* Norwood, NJ: Ablex.

Holland, J., Holyoak, K. J., Nisbett, R. E. and Thagard, P. (1986). *Induction: Process of learning, inference, and discovery.* Cambridge, MA: MIT Press.

Holyoak, K. J. (1985). The pragmatics of analogical transfer. *Psychological Learning and Motivation, 19*, 59–87.

____. (1991). Symbolic connectionism: Toward third-generation theories of expertise. In K. A. Ericsson and J. Smith (Eds.), *Toward a general theory of expertise: Prospects and limits.* Cambridge: Cambridge University Press.

Holyoak, K. J. and Glass, A. L. (1975). The role of contradictions and counterexamples in the rejection of false sentences. *Journal of Verbal Learning and Verbal Behavior, 14*, 215–239.

Holyoak, K. J. and Koh, K. (1987). Surface and structural similarity in analogical transfer. *Memory and Cognition, 15*, 332–340.

Holyoak, K. J., Novick, L. R. and Melz, E. R. (1993). Component processes in analogical transfer: Mapping, pattern completion, and adaptation. In K. J. Holyoak and J. A. Barnden (Eds.), *Advances in connectionist and neural computation theory: Vol. 2: Analogical connections.* Norwood, NJ: Ablex.

Holyoak, K. J. and Spellman, B. A. (1993). Thinking. *Annual Review of Psychology, 44*, 265–315.

Holyoak, K. J. and Thagard, P. (1989). Analogical mapping by constraint satisfaction. *Cognitive Science, 13*, 295–355.

Hsu, W., Prietula, M. and Steier, D. (1988). Merl-SOAR: Applying SOAR to scheduling. In *Proceedings Workshop on Artificial Intelligence Simulation, AAAI-88* (pp. 81–84), St. Paul, MN.

Hummel, J. E. and Holyoak, K. J. (1992). Indirect analogical mapping. In *Proceedings of the 14th Annual Conference of the Cognitive Science Society* (pp. 516—521). Hillsdale, NJ: Erlbaum.

Hunt, E. (1989). Cognitive science: Definition, status, and questions. *Annual Review of Psychology, 40*, 603–630.

Jaskowski, S. (1934). On the rules of supposition in formal logic. *Studia Logica, 1*, 5–32.

Johnson-Laird, P. N. (1983). *Mental models.* Cambridge, MA: Harvard University Press.

____. (1988). Reasoning by rule or model? In *Proceedings Tenth Annual Conference of the Cognitive Science Society* (pp. 765–771). Montreal, Quebec.

Johnson-Laird, P. N., Lengrenzi, P. and Lengrenzi, M. S. (1972). Reasoning and a sense of reality. *British Journal of Psychology, 24*, 395–400.

Just, M. A. and Carpenter, P. A. (1987). *The psychology of reading and language comprehension.* Boston, MA: Allyn and Bacon.

Kahneman, D. and Miller, D. T. (1986). Knowledge-based causal attribution: The abnormal conditions focus model. *Psychological Review, 93*, 75–88.

Kant, I. (1781). *Prolegomena to any future metaphysics.* New York: Random House.

____. (1958). *Critique of pure reason* (N. Kemp Smith, Trans.). New York: Random House. (Original work published in 1781.)

Kedar-Cabelli, S. (1985). Purpose-directed analogy. In *Proceedings Seventh Annual Conference of Cognitive Science Society* (pp. 150–159). Irvine, CA.

Kepler, J. (1937). De Motibus Stellae Martis. In *Johannes Kepler Gesammelte Werks.* Munchen: Ch. Beck.

Keyes, R. W. (1993). The future of the transistor. *Scientific American, 268*, 70–78.

Kintsch, W. (1988). The role of knowledge in discourse comprehension: A construction-integration model. *Psychological Review, 95*, 163–182.

Kirsh, D. (1991). Foundations of AI: The big issues. *Artificial Intelligence, 47*, 3–30.

Kittay, E. (1987). *Metaphor: Its cognitive force and linguistic structure.* Oxford: Clarendon Press.

Klaczynski, P. A., Gelfand, H. and Reese, H. W. (1989). Transfer of conditional reasoning: Effects of explanations and initial problem types. *Memory and Cognition, 17*, 208–220.

Kline, M. (1985). *Mathematics and the search for knowledge* (p. 144). New York: Oxford University Press.

Kling, R. E. (1971). *Reasoning by analogy with applications to heuristic problem solving: A case study.* Unpublished Ph.D. dissertation, Stanford University.

Kolata, G. (1993, June 24). At last, shout of "Eureka" in age-old math mystery. *New York Times*, p. 1.

Kolodner, J. L. (1983a). Towards an understanding of the role of experience in the evolution from novice to expert. *International Journal of Man-Machine Studies, 19*, 497–518.

____. (1983b). Maintaining order in a dynamic long-term memory. *Cognitive Science, 7*, 243–280.

____. (1983c). Reconstructive memory: A computer model. *Cognitive Science, 7*, 281–328.

Kolodner, J. L. (Ed.) (1988). *Proceedings DARPA workshop on case-based reasoning,* Clearwater Beach, FL.

Konolize, K. (1985). Belief and incompleteness. In J. R. Hobbs and R. Moore (Eds.), *Formal theories of the commonsense world.* Norwood, NJ: Ablex.

Kosko, B. (1991). *Neural networks and fuzzy systems*. Englewood Cliffs, NJ: Prentice-Hall.

Kosko, B. and Isaka, S. (1993). Fuzzy logic. *Scientific American, 269*, 76–81.

Kowalski, R. (1979). *Logic for problem solving*. Amsterdam: North-Holland.

Kulkarni, D. and Simon, H. A. (1988). The processes of scientific discovery: The strategy of experimentation. *Cognitive Science, 12*, 139–175.

Kurzweil, R. (1990). *The age of intelligent machines*. Cambridge, MA: MIT Press.

Laird, J. E. (1983). *Universal subgoaling*. Unpublished Ph.D. dissertation, Carnegie-Mellon University.

____. (1986). *SOAR's user's manual (version 4)* (Tech Rep No. ISL-15). Palo Alto, CA: Xerox Palo Alto Research Center.

____. (1988). Recovery from incorrect knowledge in SOAR. In *Proceedings AAAI-88* (pp. 618–623). St. Paul, MN.

Laird, J. E. and Newell, A. (1983). *A universal weak method* (Tech Rep No 83-141). Pittsburgh, PA: Carnegie-Mellon University, Department of Computer Science.

Laird, J. E., Newell, A. and Rosenbloom, P. S. (1987). SOAR: An architecture for general intelligence. *Artificial Intelligence, 33*, 1–64.

Laird, J. E., Rosenbloom, P. S. and Newell, A. (1984). Towards chunking as a general learning mechanism. In *Proceedings AAAI-84* (pp. 188–192). Austin, TX.

____. (1986). Chunking in SOAR: The anatomy of a general learning mechanism. *Machine Learning, 1*, 11–46.

Langley, P. (1981). Data-driven discovery of physical laws. *Cognitive Science, 5*, 31–54.

Langley, P. and Neches, R. (1981). *PRISM user's manual* (Tech Rep). Pittsburgh, PA: University of Pittsburgh, Department of Psychology.

Langley, P., Simon, H. A., Bradshaw, G. L. and Zytkow, J. M. (1987). *Scientific discovery: Computational explorations of the creative processes*. Cambridge, MA: MIT Press.

Larkin, J. H., McDermott, J., Simon, D. P. and Simon, H. A. (1980). Models of competence in solving physics problems. *Cognitive Science, 4*, 317–345.

Larkin, J. H., Reif, F., Carbonell, J. and Gugliotta, A. (1988). FERMI: A flexible expert reasoner with multi-domain inferencing. *Cognitive Science, 12*, 101–138.

Leahey, T. and Wagman, M. (1974). The modification of fallacious reasoning with implication. *Journal of General Psychology, 91*, 277–285.

Lenat, D. B. (1976). AM: An artificial intelligence approach to discovery in mathematics as heuristic search. Ph.D. dissertation, Stanford University.

Lenat, D. B. and Feigenbaum, E. A. (1991). On the thresholds of knowledge. *Artificial Intelligence, 47*, 185–250.

Lenat, D. B. and Guha, R. B. (1989). *Building large knowledge-based systems, representation, and inference in the eye project*. Reading, MA: Addison Wesley.

Levesque, H. J. (1986). Knowledge representation and reasoning. In *Annual Review of Computer Science 1* (pp. 255–287). Palo Alto, CA: Annual Reviews Inc.

Lewis, R. L., Newell, A. and Polk. T. A. (1989). Toward a SOAR theory of taking instructions for immediate reasoning tasks. In *Proceedings Eleventh Annual Conference of the Cognitive Science Society*, Ann Arbor, MI.

Locke, J. (1975). *An essay concerning human understanding* (P. H. Nidditch, Ed.), Oxford: Clarendon Press. (Original work published in 1690.)

Logan, G. D. (1988). Toward an instance theory of automatization. *Psychological Review, 95,* 492–527.

Lucas, J. R. (1961). Minds, machines, and Gödel. *Philosophy, 36,* 112–127.

Lunzer, E. A., Harrison, C. and Davey, M. (1972). The four-card selection problem and generality of formal reasoning. *Quarterly Journal of Experimental Psychology, 24,* 326–339.

Macnamara, J. (1986). *A border dispute: The place of logic in psychology.* Cambridge, MA: MIT Press.

Malgady, R. G. and Johnson, M. G. (1980). Measurement of figurative language: Semantic feature models of comprehension and appreciation. In R. P. Honeck and R. R. Hoffman (Eds.), *Cognition and figurative language* (pp. 239–258). Hillsdale, NJ: Erlbaum.

Mannes, S. M. and Kintsch, W. (1991). Routine computing tasks: Planning as understanding. *Cognitive Science, 115,* 305–342.

Martin, L. (1986). Eskimo words for snow: A case study on the genesis and decay of an anthropological example. *American Anthropologist, 88,* 418–423.

McClelland, J. L., Rumelhart, D. E., and the PDP Research Group (Eds.) (1986). *Parallel distributed processing: Explorations in the microstructure of cognition 2: Psychological and biological models.* Cambridge, MA: MIT Press/Bradford Books.

McDermott, D. (1990). A critique of pure reason. In M. Boden (Ed.), *The philosophy of artificial intelligence* (pp. 206–230). Oxford: Oxford University Press.

McDermott, J. (1978). *ANA: An assimilating and accomodating production system* (Tech Rep No. CMU-CS-78-156). Pittsburgh, PA: Carnegie-Mellon University, Computer Science Department.

____. (1979). Learning to use analogies. In *Proceedings IJCAI-79* (pp. 568–576). Tokyo.

Miller, G. A. (1956). The magical number seven, plus or minus two: Some limits on our capacity for processing information. *Psychological Review, 63,* 81–97.

Minsky, M. (1975). A framework for the representation of knowledge. In P. Winston (Ed.), *The psychology of computer vision.* New York: McGraw-Hill.

____. (1986). *The society of mind.* New York: Simon and Schuster.

____. (1991). Logical versus analogical or symbolic versus connectionist or neat versus scruffy. *AI Magazine, 12,* 34–51.

Mitchell, T. M. (1982). Generalization as search. *Artificial Intelligence, 18,* 203–226.

Mitchell, T. M., Keller, R. M. and Kedar-Cabelli, S. T. (1986). Explanation-based generalization: A unifying view. *Machine Learning, 1,* 47–80.

Mitchell, T. M., Utgoff, P. E. and Banerji, R. (1983). Learning by experimentation: Acquiring and refining problem-solving heuristics. In R. Michalski, J. G. Carbonell and T. M. Mitchell (Eds.), *Machine learning: An artificial intelligence approach* (pp. 163–190). Palo Alto, CA: Tioga.

Montague, R. (1974). *Formal philosophy: Selected papers of Richard Montague* (R. H. Thomason, Ed.). New Haven, CT: Yale University Press.

Munyer, J. C. (1981). *Analogy as a means of discovery in problem solving and learning.* Ph.D. dissertation, University of California.

Newell, A. (1980). Reasoning, problem solving, and decision processes: The problem space as a fundamental category. In R. Nickerson (Ed.), *Attention and Performance 8.* Hillsdale, NJ: Erlbaum.

____. (1990) *Unified theories of cognition.* Cambridge, MA: Harvard University Press.

____. (1991). Unified theories of cognition: The William James lectures. Manuscript.

Newell, A. and Rosenbloom, P. S. (1981). Mechanisms of skill acquisition and the law of practice. In J. R. Anderson (Ed.), *Cognitive skills and their acquisition* (pp. 1–55). Hillsdale, NJ: Erlbaum.

Newell, A. and Simon, H. A. (1972). *Human problem solving.* Englewood Cliffs, NJ: Prentice Hall.

Newell, A., Rosenbloom, P. S. and Laird, J. E. (1989). Symbolic architectures for cognition. In M. I. Posner (Ed.), *Foundations of Cognitive Science.* Cambridge, MA: MIT Press/Bradford Books.

Nilsson, N. J. (1980). *Principles of artificial intelligence.* Palo Alto, CA: Tioga.

____. (1991). Logic and artificial intelligence. *Artificial Intelligence, 47,* 31–56.

Norman, D. A. (1991). Approaches to the study of intelligence. *Artificial Intelligence, 47,* 327–346.

Osherson, D. N. (1974–1976). *Logical abilities in children* (Vol. 2–4). Hillsdale, NJ: Erlbaum.

Osherson, D. N. and Smith, E. E. (1981). On the adequacy of prototype theory as a theory of concepts. *Cognition, 9,* 35–58.

____. (1982). Gradedness and conceptual combination. *Cognition, 12,* 299–318.

Owen, E., and Sweller, J. (1985). What do students learn while solving mathematics problems? *Journal of Educational Psychology, 77,* 272–284.

Partridge, D. and Wilkes, Y. (Eds.) (1990). *The foundations of AI: A sourcebook.* Cambridge: Cambridge University Press.

Pirolli, P. L. and Anderson, J. R. (1985). The role of learning from examples in the acquisition of recursive programming skills. *Canadian Journal of Psychology, 39,* 240–272.

Plato (1956). Meno. In E. H. Wormington and P. O. Rouse (Eds.), *Great dialogues of Plato.* (W. H. D. Rouse, Trans.). New York: New American Library.

Polk, T. A. and Newell, A. (1988). Modeling human syllogistic reasoning in SOAR. In *Proceedings Tenth Annual Conference of the Cognitive Science Society* (pp. 181–187). Montreal.

Pollard, P. (1982). Human reasoning: Some possible effects of availability. *Cognition, 12,* 65–96.

Post, E. L. (1943). Formal reductions of the general combinatorial decision problem. *American Journal of Mathematics, 65,* 197–268.

Powell, L. (1984). *Parsing the picnic problem with SOAR3 implementation of Dypar-3.* Pittsburgh, PA: Carnegie-Mellon University, Department of Computer Science.

Prenowitz, W. and Jordon, M. (1965). *Basic concepts of geometry.* New York: Cambridge University Press.

Pullman, G. K. (1989). The great Eskimo vocabulary hoax. *National Language and Linguistic Theory, 7,* 275–281.

Qin, Y. and Simon, H. A. (1990). Laboratory replication of scientific discovery processes. *Cognitive Science, 14,* 281–312.

Quine, W. V. O. (1960). *Word and object.* Cambridge, MA: MIT Press.

____. (1961). *From a logical point of view* (2d ed.). New York: Harper Torchbooks.

Quinlan, J. R. (1986). Induction of decision trees. *Machine Learning, 1,* 81–106.

Rajamoney, S., DeJong, G. F. and Faltings, B. (1985). Towards a model of conceptual knowledge acquisition through directed experimentation. In *Proceedings IJCAI-85* (pp. 688–690). Los Angeles, CA.

Ranney, M. (1993). Explorations in explanatory coherence. In E. Bar-On, B. Eylon and Z. Schertz (Eds.), *Designing intelligent learning environments: From cognitive analysis to computer implementation*. Norwood, NJ: Ablex.

Read, S. J. and Marcus-Newhall, A. (1993). The role of explanatory coherence in social explanations. *Journal of Personality and Social Psychology*. In press.

Reich, Y. (1988). *Learning plans as a weak method for design*. Pittsburgh, PA: Carnegie-Mellon University, Department of Civil Engineering.

Rich, E. and Knight, K. (1991). *Artificial intelligence* (2d ed.). New York: McGraw-Hill.

Riemann, B. (1953). *Gesammelte mathematische Werke*, 2d ed. (pp. 272–87, 391–404). New York: Dover (Reprint).

Rips, L. J. (1983). Cognitive processes in propositional reasoning. *Psychological Review*, *90*, 38–71.

____. (1984). Reasoning as a central intellective ability. In R. J. Sternberg (Ed.), *The representation of knowledge and belief* (pp. 258–286). Tucson: University of Arizona Press.

____. (1986). Mental muddles. In M. Brand and R. M. Harnish (Eds.), *The representation of knowledge and belief* (pp. 258–286). Tucson: University of Arizona Press.

____. (1989). The psychology of knights and knaves. *Cognition*, *31*, 85–116.

Rips, L. J. and Conrad, F. G. (1983). Individual differences in deduction? *Cognition and Brain Theory*, *6*, 259–285.

Robinson, J. A. (1965). A machine-oriented logic based on the resolution principle. *Journal of the Association for Computing Machinery*, *12*, 23–41.

Rosenbloom, P. S. (1988). Beyond generalization as search: Towards a unified framework for the acquisition of new knowledge. In G. F. DeJong (Ed.), *Proceedings AAAI Symposium on Explanation-Based Learning* (pp. 17–21). Stanford, CA.

____. (1989). A symbolic goal-oriented perspective on connectionism and SOAR. In R. Pfeifer, Z. Schreter, F. Fogelman-Soulie and L. Steels (Eds.), *Connectionism in perspective*. Amsterdam: Elsevier.

Rosenbloom, P. S. and Laird, J. E. (1986). Mapping explanation-based generalization onto SOAR. In *Proceedings AAAI-86* (pp. 561–567). Philadelphia, PA.

Rosenbloom, P. S., Laird, J. E., McDermott, J., Newell, A. and Orciuch, E. (1985). R1-SOAR: An experiment in knowledge-intensive programming in a problem-solving architecture. *IEEE Transactions on Pattern Analysis and Machine Intelligence*, *7*, 561–569.

Rosenbloom, P. S., Laird, J. E. and Newell, A. (1987). Knowledge level learning in SOAR. In *Proceedings AAAI-87* (pp. 499–504). Seattle, WA.

____. (1988). The chunking of skill and knowledge. In B. A. G. Elsendoorn and H. Bouma (Eds.), *Working models of human perception*. London: Academic Press.

Rosenbloom, P. S., Laird, J. E., Newell, A. and McCarl, R. (1991). A preliminary analysis of the SOAR architecture as a basis for general intelligence. *Artificial Intelligence*, *47*, 289–325.

Rosenbloom, P. S. and Newell, A. (1986). The chunking of goal hierarchies: A generalized model of practice. In R. S. Michalski, J. G. Carbonnell and T. M. Mitchell (Eds.), *Machine learning: An artificial intelligence approach 2*. Los Altos, CA: Morgan Kaufmann.

Rosenbloom, P. S., Newell, A. and Laird, J. E. (1990). Towards the knowledge level in SOAR: The role of the architecture in the use of knowledge. In K. VanLehn (Ed.), *Architectures for intelligence*. Hillsdale, NJ: Erlbaum.

Rosenschein, S. J. and Kaebling, L. P. (1986). The synthesis of machines with provably epistemic properties. In J. Y. Halpern (Ed.), *Proceedings of the 1986 Conference on Aspects of Reasoning about Knowledge* (pp. 83–98). Los Altos, CA: Morgan Kaufmann.

Rumelhart, D. E., McClelland, J. L. and the PDP Research Group (Eds.) (1986). *Parallel distributed processing: Explorations in the microstructure of cognition 1: Foundations*. Cambridge, MA: MIT Press/Bradford Books.

Rychlak, J. F. (1990). *Artificial intelligence and human reason: A teleological critique*. New York: New York University Press.

Sacerdoti, E. D. (1974). Planning in a hierarchy of abstraction spaces. *Artificial Intelligence*, *5*, 115–135.

Saul, R. H. (1984). *A SOAR2 implementation of version-space inductive learning*. Pittsburgh, PA: Carnegie-Mellon University, Computer Science Department.

Schank, P. and Ranney, M. (1991). The psychological fidelity of ECHO: Modeling an experimental study of explanatory coherence. In *Proceedings of 13th Annual Conference of the Cognitive Science Society* (pp. 892–897). Hillsdale, NJ: Erlbaum.

____. (1992). Accessing explanatory coherence: A new method for integrating verbal data with models of on-line brief revision. In *Proceedings of the 14th Annual Conference of the Cognitive Science Society* (pp. 599–604). Hillsdale, NJ: Erlbaum.

Schank, R. C. (1982). *Dynamic memory: A theory of reminding and learning in computers and people*. London: Cambridge University.

____. (1985). *Dynamic memory*. Hillsdale, NJ: Erlbaum.

Schank, R., and Ableson, R. (1977). *Scripts, plans, goals and understanding*. Hillsdale, NJ: Erlbaum.

Schank, R. C. and Riesbeck, C. (1981). *Inside computer understanding*. Hillsdale, NJ: Erlbaum.

Seller, J., Mawer, R. and Ward, M. (1983). Development of expertise in mathematical problem solving. *Journal of Experimental Psychology: General*, *112*, 639–661.

Shastri, L. and Ajjangadde, V. (1993). From simple associations to systematic reasoning: A connectionist representation of rules, variables and dynamic bindings. *Behavior and Brain Sciences*, *16*, 118–129.

Simon, H. A. (1979). Artificial intelligence research strategies in the light of artificial intelligence models of scientific discovery. *Proceedings of the Sixth International Joint Conference on Artificial Intelligence* (pp. 1086–1094). Los Angeles, CA.

____. (1990). Invariants of human behavior. *Annual Review of Psychology*, *41*, 1–20.

Simpson, R. L. (1985). *A computer model of case-based reasoning in problem solving: An investigation in the domain of dispute mediation*. Unpublished Ph.D. dissertation, Georgia Institute of Technology.

Smith, E. E., Langston, C. and Nisbett, R. E. (1992). The case for rules in reasoning. *Cognitive Science, 16*, 1–40.

Smith, E. E., Shoben, E. J. and Rips, L. J. (1974). Structure and process in semantic memory: A featural model for semantic decisions. *Psychological Review, 81*, 214–241.

Smolensky, P. (1988). On the proper treatment of connectionism. *Behavior and Brain Science, 11*, 1–23.

Smullyan, R. M. (1978). *What is the name of this book? The riddle of Dracula and other logical puzzles.* Englewood Cliffs, NJ: Prentice-Hall.

Spellman, B. A. and Holyoak, K. J. (1992). If Saddam is Hitler then who is George Bush? Analogical mapping between systems of social roles. *Journal of Personality and Social Psychology, 62*, 913–933.

Stallman, R. M. and Sussman, G. J. (1977). Forward reasoning and dependency-directed backtracking in a system for computer-aided circuit design. *Artificial Intelligence, 9*, 135–196.

Steier, D. (1987). Cypress-SOAR: A case study in search and learning in algorithm design. In *Proceedings IJCAI-87* (pp. 327–330). Milan, Italy.

Steier, D. M., Laird, J. E., Newell, A., Rosenbloom, P. S., Flynn, R., Goldirig, A., Polk, T. A., Shivers, O. G., Unruh, A., and Yost, G. R. (1987). Varieties of learning in SOAR, 1987. In P. Langley (Ed.), *Proceedings Fourth International Workshop on Machine Learning* (pp. 300–311). Irvine, CA.

Steier, D. M. and Newell, A. (1988). Integrating multiple sources of knowledge in Designer-SOAR: An automatic algorithm designer. In *Proceedings AAAI-88* (pp. 8–13). St. Paul, MN.

Stenning, K. and Levy, J. (1988). Knowledge-rich solutions to the binding problem: A simulation of some human computational mechanisms. *Knowledge Based Systems, 1*, 143–152.

Stenning, K. and Oaksford, M. (1993). Rational reasoning and human implementations of logics. In K. I. Manktelow and D. E. Over (Eds.), *Rationality*. London: Routledge.

Stenning, K., Shepherd, M. and Levy, J. (1988). On the construction of representations for individuals from descriptions in text. *Language and Cognitive Processes, 2*, 129–164.

Sternberg, R. J. (1977). *Intelligence, information processing, and analogical reasoning: The componential analysis of human abilities.* Hillsdale, NJ: Erlbaum.

Sweller, J. (1988). Cognitive load during problem solving: Effects on learning. *Cognitive Science, 12*, 247–285.

Tambe, M. (1988). *Speculations on the computational effects of chunking.* Pittsburgh, PA: Carnegie-Mellon University, Computer Science Department.

Tambe, M., Acharya, A. and Gupta, A. (1989). *Implementation of production systems on message passing computers: Simulation results and analysis* (Tech Rep No CMU-CS-89-129). Pittsburgh, PA: Carnegie-Mellon University, School of Computer Science.

Tambe, M., Kalp, D., Gupta, A., Forgy, C. L., Milnes, B. and Newell, A. (1988). SOAR/PSM-E: Investigating mass parallelism in a learning production system. In *Proceedings ACM/SIGPLAN Symposium on Parallel Programming:*

Experience with Applications, Languages, and Systems (pp. 146–161). Atlanta, GA.

Tambe, M. and Newell, A. (1988). Some chunks are expensive. In J. Laird (Ed.), *Proceedings Fifth International Conference on Machine Learning* (pp. 451–458). Ann Arbor, MI.

Tambe, M. and Rosenbloom, P. S. (1989). Eliminating expensive chunks by restricting expressiveness. In *Proceedings IJCAI-89*, Detroit, MI.

Taraban, R. and McClelland, J. L. (1988). Constituent attachment and thematic role assignment in sentence processing: Influences of content-based expectations. *Journal of Memory and Language, 27*, 597–632.

Thagard, P. (1989). Explanatory coherence. *Behavioral and Brain Sciences, 12*, 435–467.

____. (1992). *Conceptual revolutions.* Princeton, NJ: Princeton University Press.

Thagard, P., Holyoak, K. J., Nelson, G. and Gochfeld, D. (1990). Analog retrieval by constraint satisfaction. *Artificial Intelligence, 46*, 259–310.

Turing, A. (1936). On computable numbers, with an application to Entscheudungs problem. *Proceedings of the London Mathematics Society, 52*, 230–265.

____. (1950). Computing machinery and intelligence. *Mind, 59*, 434–460.

Turing, A. M. (1963). Computing machinery and intelligence. In E. A. Feigenbaum and J. Feldman (Eds.), *Computers and thought.* New York: McGraw-Hill. (Original work published in 1950.)

Tweney, R. D. (1990). Five questions for computationalists. In J. Shrager and P. Langley (Eds.), *Computational models of scientific discovery and theory formation* (pp. 471–484). San Mateo, CA: Morgan Kaufmann.

Unruh, A. and Rosenbloom, P. S. (1989). Abstraction in problem solving and learning. In *Proceedings IJCAI-89*, Detroit, MI.

Unruh, A., Rosenbloom, P. S. and Laird, J. E. (1987). Dynamic abstraction problem solving in SOAR. In *Proceedings Third Annual Aerospace Applications of Artificial Intelligence Conference* (pp. 245–256). Dayton, OH.

Wagman, M. (1978). The comparative effects of didactic-correction and self-contradiction on fallacious scientific and personal reasoning. *Journal of General Psychology, 99*, 31–39.

____. (1979). Systematic dilemma counseling: Theory, method, research. *Psychological Reports, 44*, 55–72.

____. (1980). PLATO DCS, an interactive computer system for personal counseling. *Journal of Counseling Psychology, 27*, 16–30.

____. (1984). *The dilemma and the computer: Theory, research, and applications to counseling psychology.* New York: Praeger.

____. (1988). *Computer psychotherapy systems: Theory and research foundations.* New York: Gordon & Breach.

____. (1991a). *Artificial intelligence and human cognition: A theoretical intercomparison of two realms of intellect.* Westport, CT: Praeger.

____. (1991b). *Cognitive science and concepts of mind: Toward a general theory of human and artificial intelligence.* Westport, CT: Praeger.

____. (1993). *Cognitive psychology and artificial intelligence: Theory and research in cognitive science.* Westport, CT: Praeger.

Wagman, M. and Kerber, K. W. (1980). PLATO DCS, an interactive computer system for personal counseling: Further development and evaluation. *Journal of*

Counseling Psychology, 27, 31–39.

Washington, R. and Rosenbloom, P. S. (1988). *Applying problem solving and learning to diagnosis*. Stanford, CA: Stanford University Press.

Wason, P. C. (1966). Reasoning. In B. Foss (Ed.), *New horizons in psychology*. Harmondsworth: Penguin Books.

Wason, P. C. and Green, D. W. (1984). Reasoning and mental representation. *Quarterly Journal of Experimental Psychology*, *36A*, 597–610.

Wason, P. C. and Johnson-Laird, P. N. (1972). *The psychology of reasoning*. Cambridge, MA: Harvard University Press.

Wason, P. C. and Shapiro, D. (1971). Natural and contrived experience in a reasoning problem. *Quarterly Journal of Experimental Psychology*, *23*, 63–71.

Weismeyer, M. (1988). *SOAR I/O reference manual, version 2*. Ann Arbor: University of Michigan, Department of EECS.

____. (1989). *New and improved SOAR I/O*. Ann Arbor: University of Michigan, Department of EECS.

Whorf, B. (1956). *Language, thought, and reality* (J. Carroll, Ed.), Cambridge, MA: MIT Press.

Winston, P. H. (1975). Learning structural descriptions from examples. In P. H. Winston (Ed.), *The Psychology of Computer Vision*. New York: McGraw-Hill.

____. (1978). Learning by creating and justifying transfer frames. *Artificial Intelligence*, *10*, 147–172.

____. (1980). Learning and reasoning by analogy. *Communication ACM*, *23*, 689–703.

____. (1982). Learning new principles from precedents and exercises. *Artificial Intelligence*, *19*, 321–350.

____. (1983). Learning by augmenting rules and accumulating censors. In *Proceedings International Machine Learning Workshop* (pp. 2–11). Monticello, IL.

____. (1984). *Artificial Intelligence*. Reading, MA: Addison-Wesley.

____. (1986). Learning by augmenting rules and accumulating censors. In R. S. Michalski, J. G. Carbonell and T. M. Mitchell (Eds.), *Machine learning: An artificial intelligence approach* (pp. 45–61). Los Altos, CA: Morgan Kaufmann.

Winston, P. H., Binford, T. O., Katz, B. and Lowry, M. (1983). Learning physical descriptions from functional definitions. In *Proceedings AAAI-83* (pp. 433–439). Washington, DC.

Yager, R. R. (Ed.) (1987). *Fuzzy sets and applications; Selected papers by L. A. Zadeh*. New York: Wiley-Interscience.

Zadeh, L. A. (1979). A theory of approximate reasoning. In J. Hayes, D. Michie and L. I. Mikulich (Eds.), *Machine Intelligence 9* (pp. 149–194). New York: Halstead Press.

Author Index

Subject Index

ABOUT THE AUTHOR

MORTON WAGMAN is Professor Emeritus of Psychology at the University of Illinois, Urbana-Champaign. He has published widely including the Praeger titles *The Dilemma and the Computer* (1984); *Artificial Intelligence and Human Cognition* (1991); *Cognitive Science and Concepts of Mind* (1991); *Cognitive Psychology and Artificial Intelligence* (1993).

ISBN 0-275-94948-6

HARDCOVER BAR CODE